MISERABLE YOU™

A HANDY GUIDE TO UNHAPPINESS YOU'RE ALREADY FOLLOWING

INTERNATIONAL LIFE & BUSINESS COACH
AND AWARD-WINNING WRITER

RON MILETI

MISERABLE YOU™

A Handy Guide To Unhappiness You're Already Following.

International Life & Business Coach
And Award-Winning Writer

Ron Mileti

Published by

Hardcover ISBN: 979-8-9891256-0-9
Library of Congress Control Number: 2023917221

Paperback ISBN: 979-8-9891256-1-6

E-Book ISBN: 979-8-9891256-2-3

First edition 2023

Creative Direction by Ron Mileti and Maya Mileti
Book Design by Maya Mileti
Illustrations in part by Roman Lysenko, created in an occupied territory
during the Ukraine War
Typography: Hand-drawn font by Maya Mileti, text font EB Garamond,
Mulish.

Sucker Punch Life LLC
Scottsdale, Arizona

Visit us on the web: www.miserableyou.com and www.suckerpunchlife.com

Dedication

This book is dedicated to all the people who have tried to make a difference in your life and help you be (ugh) happy. The saps! Their efforts have been noble, but wonderfully ineffective. Yowzah, just look at how miserable you are!

This book is also dedicated to YOU! You've demonstrated a remarkable commitment to ignoring input from others and hitting yourself in the head over and over again with a proverbial sledgehammer. Keep up the good work, miserable you!

"Table It" Of Contents

Introduction

Maybe you're hap-hap-happy with how things are going in your life. Or maybe you feel "meh", like something is missing. Or maybe you're so frustrated you want to flip a table or twelve. Wherever you're at, whatever you're feeling, I say the real issue is **YOU'RE NOT MISERABLE ENOUGH!**

That's why I'm here to guide you step-by-step to an utterly, wonderfully, beautifully miserable life! **You've been dabbling in misery long enough. Let's level up your game and really get into the muck!**

I'll admit it. I've tried to help many people be happier (my fingers cramped up just typing that!). As a **Life Coach & Business Trainer with a prestigious international organization** (you're welcome), I've led thousands of coaching sessions, with hundreds of people all over the world, from Australia to Switzerland to Saudi Arabia to the United States to Bermuda. Many people did get happier. Lots happier.

Some however were stuck in their miserable ways. This book is for everyone, but especially for those who can't figure out how to get happy. I wrote this how-to book particularly for those who say, "I'm fine thanks" but have no passion for life. The ambitiously joyless. The perpetually annoyed. The frequently upset. The committedly miserable. **I wrote this book so you, dear reader, can finally master the art of being miserable. You've been an amateur for years. It's time to go pro!**

Sure, this book may have the opposite effect on you. It might finally bitch-slap you awake. You might finally realize that this is your one and only life, and you better get to the smiling already. However, let's avoid this!

So if you're truly committed to suffering (from those inch-deep wrinkles on your forehead, seems like you are!), then read on and discover how you're already making yourself miserable, and what steps you can take to make yourself even more wretched!

Or, if you insist, instead you can use this book to discover what self-torture you've been unconsciously using on yourself, learn how to stop doing that, and finally be (ugh) happy. But what a wussy move that would be!

Either way, if you're able to turn the page while in that mental stockade you put yourself in, let's begin!

IN THE MOVIE *ROCKY*, THE THEME SONG SAYS "GONNA FLY NOW." SO ROCKY RAN FAST IN THE STREETS. BUT HE NEVER FLEW. GEESH, TRY HARDER NEXT TIME, ROCKY!

Lesson 1:

Start Many Things. Finish Nothing.

L et's face it, living a life of misery takes commitment, focus, hard-headiness, and a little old-fashioned gumption. But with some discipline and effort, you can reach an even more complete, all-encompassing, ever-present, long-sustained level of misery. YOU GOT THIS, MY MISERABLE FRIEND!

As an example, if you're truly committed to being miserable (and from the looks of things over there, you are!), then you may already practice the habit of starting many things and finishing not one of them. Zip. Nada. (For instance, how's that bedazzling business coming along, hmm?)

Is there something you've been wanting to do? Start a new career? Ask that girl on a date? Finish a sentence? To continue to be miserable, just ignore those urges. Give into that little voice that says "don't bother." Come on, you know you wanna give up. It's best not to start the effort at all, right? But if you do start, all is not lost, you can simply quit with a whimper and a "never mind" and a "I didn't really want that stupid thing anyway"!

The good news? There are knowable, learnable steps to forming this get-nowhere, start-stop, on-again off-again habit of finishing nothing you start. The steps are simple to master (if you can stay awake long enough to follow them):

How to Finish Nothing:

- **First, get excited about something.** Anything. Whatever. The latest shiny object. Yoga. Keto. A new job. Self-respect.
- **Next, rather than starting, buy lots of stuff related to your new activity, because it's easier than actually starting.** Yoga stretchy pants. Crazy-priced frozen keto meals. A new designer suit for work. This book.
- **Then...here's the fun part...don't get into action.** Don't follow through. Leave that new stuff in the box. Wait for Divine Forces to motivate you to take action (spoiler alert: they won't).
- **In other words, give into your feeling that you don't wanna start.** Don't make a simple, rational, left-brained choice to simply BEGIN! Don't simply get in action even though you don't feel like it, even though you're tired, even though it's easier to binge-scroll through the Netflix menu for an hour (what exactly do they mean by the category "Casual Viewing" anyway? Are some people looking for "Prim and Proper Viewing"?!)

People think motivation comes first, then action. Research studies (I'm too lazy to note whose) have shown the opposite is true: people get into action as a rational decision, then once in action, after a few minutes of activity, they start feeling motivated and wonder "Hey, why don't I do this thing more often?!"

In other words, most people believe it works like this:
- **Feel Motivated —> Get In Action**

Here's how it really works:
- **Get In Action —> Feel Motivated**

This is good news for you if you don't want to actually get moving: you'll never feel like it! So ignore that voice in the rational part of your mind that's screaming to just get started. Don't make the decision to begin from your commitments, make the decision from your feelings. You'll get started when you feel like it...which will likely be never! More chips?

Being in action is scary. Risky. You could fail! Plus it requires effort. Energy. Stop that. Relax. Rest. Your couch is soft and squishy, so sit on it and soon you'll share those qualities. If you're really committed to being miserable (and clearly you are, right?), you'll want to make your couch your best friend. Your couch has your back...on its face.

> "Only put off until tomorrow what you are willing to die having left undone."
> - Pablo Picasso

> "Hey Pablo, less talky talky, more painty painty!"
> - Me

So start many things with a gung-ho attitude, then, leave them half...

NOTES

Write Your Notes Here
(Then immediately forget about them like you always do. HA!)

_____

_____

_____

_____

_____

_____

_____

_____

_____

_____

_____

_____

_____

_____

_____

IT TAKES MORE MUSCLES TO FROWN THAN SMILE. IT TAKES EVEN MORE MUSCLES TO WALK AWAY FROM YOUR SMARMY ASS.

SMiLE

12 MUSCLES USED

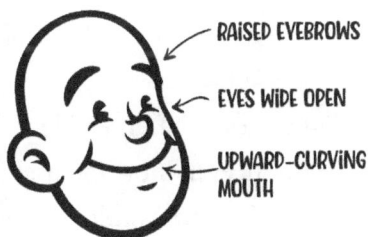

RAiSED EYEBROWS

EYES WiDE OPEN

UPWARD-CURViNG MOUTH

FROWN

47 MUSCLES USED

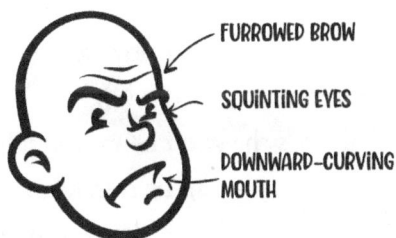

FURROWED BROW

SQUiNTiNG EYES

DOWNWARD-CURViNG MOUTH

Lesson 2:

Be In A Bad Mood Often

You've got plenty to be miserable about, right? Your life sucks ass, correct? **You DESERVE to be disappointed or furious or sad or jaded or have no discernable emotions at all like the walking dead.** Your broke-ass life gives you EVERY RIGHT to abuse the waiter, run that a-hole off the road, and give the silent treatment to your spouse (love schmuv!). Enjoy your misery. Sip it like a fine wine. You've earned it.

Here's the good news: though you might already be miserable occasionally, you can be miserable even more often, even more intensely. **You, yes YOU, can develop mad skills at being miserable.** Like a ninja of self-inflicted pain. A karate chop to your own head! Ready to develop some skills, so you can deepen those down days, lower those lows, throw gas on those fires, and go nuclear with your rage?

Here are **6 Steps To Being In A Bad Mood Often**:

Step 1. First, resolve to be miserable: Commit that no matter what, you're going to make misery happen for you and others (you're generous that way). Got thoughts that maybe you should lighten up? **Feel like you need to shift into a better mood? Push those feelings down into your gut like grandma's 20-pound fruitcake!** You're right, you're justified, you're doing the best you can, it's their fault not yours! How can you be in a good mood when there's that Really Bad Thing in your life, right? When the world is perfect, and your life is perfect, then and only then will you be in a good mood!

Step 2. Look for what's wrong: There's so much wrong in the world and especially in your ho-hum life, am I right? Look for what's wrong. Find the lack. **The glass isn't just half empty, the glass has someone else's lipstick on the rim!** Look for what's wrong like a birddog on the hunt. Ignore the good things all around you (sure, there's just as much good in the world as bad, but ignore the glittery good stuff, my Wednesday Addams!). Focus on the bad. Take control of your focus, look for the crummy, and your whole world can change for the worse! Make Debbie Downer your spirit animal!

Step 3. Don't be grateful: Avoid appreciating anything in your life. Your spouse. The kids. That job that keeps your lazy-ass fed. That's all owed to you, right? How about that phone in your pocket? Years ago, that was science fiction, now it's yours, a miracle, and just a few hundred bucks! But don't be grateful for this, instead focus on the fact that the Maps app took you to the side door instead of the front entrance of that new shopping mall DAMMIT! Experience no wonder or awe. Appreciate nothing. Enjoy nada. **Experience the buffet of life like you're chewing on cardboard. Bland. Tasteless.** Don't notice what you have, focus on what you don't. There's SO MUCH you don't have, and it ALL should be yours! It's your RIGHT, right?!

Step 4. Learn nothing new. You know puh-lenty already so there's really no need to learn more or grow as a person. You are Da Man (even if you're Da Woman) and you know what's what. You're all-knowing, you're right, you're justified, there are no other points of view worth considering. Facts are overrated. Science is for wusses. Curiosity killed the cat and it's not going to kill this cat! Close that mind like a steel trap. Lock the doors and windows of your brain. **When there's an opportunity to grow and blossom, throw some Clorox bleach on that!** There's no need to learn, grow, and become "more" because you're already more/better/different than all those other a-holes out there. Wanting to grow implies that you're lacking in some way, imperfect. Shut those thoughts down! Defend who you are like a rabid unthinking animal.

Step 5. Give nothing: You worked hard for what you got. You're not going to just give it away, are you? Giving to others is for fools! Contributing to others, making a difference in their lives? Why the hell would you want to do that?! Protect your time. Hoard your skills. Hide your money. Stuff down that urge to make a difference with others (who the hell are they to you?). Tell others no, they can do that thing on their own, you don't have time to help, you're a Very Important Person (translation: Not Them). Ignore the fact that forgetting about yourself for a while and helping others is one of the quintessential ways to feel fulfilled in life. Wanting to help others in a selfless way is instinctual for us humans, and we don't feel completely happy unless we are making a difference with other people. But you and I are not interested in fulfillment, **we're interested in gathering and hoarding as much money and success and stuff** as possible, like obsessed squirrels gathering bitter, unsatisfying nuts.

Step 6. Don't celebrate the little wins: There's no need to celebrate. Any good that happens was owed to you. **No need to be thankful, excited, jump up and down, or give a woo or a hoo.** Celebrating little victories can make you feel good, sure, but it can make you believe puny incidental victories are enough. You deserve more! Life is an all-or-nothing situation,

DON'T LEARN FROM WEIRD KIDS!

My 8yo in the car today: "Do you want me to throw the confetti in my pocket?" Me: "No not in the car! - why do you have confetti in your pocket?" 8yo: "It's my emergency confetti, I carry it everywhere in case there is good news."

- Ana the Distracted Gardner @annastayshaa

my miserable friend! We don't just want a good life, we want the #1 Life Of All People Of All Time! It's not just about having money, it's about having MORE THAN EVERYONE ELSE. It's not about being attractive to someone you love, it's about being attractive to EVERY PERSON, NO EXCEPTIONS. It's not about succeeding at something, it's about STANDING ON THE TRAMPLED BODIES OF YOUR COMPETITORS! It's not about being a good and kind person, it's about being THE MOST SELFLESS AND RIGHTEOUS PERSON EVER AMEN! If you're not able to post jealousy-inducing photos on Insta all day long, making others cry from comparing themselves to you, then you've still got work to do, buckaroo. So, forget about celebrating for now, you can celebrate when you finally get to the very top of human experience, better than all people, past, present and future. Until then, keep scratching, clawing and climbing.

Bonus Step: Get Your Body Into It:

The 6 Steps To Being In A Bad Mood Often are a handy-dandy guide to training your mind to wallow in misery more intensely and more often. However, **there's another tool that can help you stay in tip-top miserable shape: your body.** Want to be miserable? Your body can help too. Here's an

A THOUGHT TO AVOID:

WHATEVER YOU DO TODAY, DO IT WITH THE CONFIDENCE OF A 4-YEAR-OLD IN A BATMAN T-SHIRT.

example: sit on your couch for hours and hours, watching hate-filled news or tragically mediocre dancers on social media. Do this while not moving, breathing shallow, expressionless, eyes glazed over, staring at the screen. Do this and bingo-bango-bongo, you're feeling lethargic, sad, depressed, and miserable! That's because what you do with your body (or don't do with your body) affects how you feel. If you want to be miserable, you'll want to avoid moving with energy, putting a big smile on your face, opening your peepers wide, pumping your arms in the air, and shouting YIPPEE in a loud voice. That will lead to icky feelings of energy, enthusiasm, and happiness. Instead, frown, point those eyebrows downward, clench your fists, grind your teeth. Use your body this way over and over again until it's habit, so you don't even notice when you're doing it, and suffering will be yours more and more often. Now that's an amazing body of work, my miserable friend!

Speaking of facial expressions, let's look at yours. Does your face tell the world to go to hell? Or does your face just hang there like some dead thing? Or does your face look like it should have a soundtrack of sad violins? If so, nice work putting on a face of misery! Whatever you do, don't put a big smile on your face! **When you smile, your brain releases molecules called neuropeptides that fight off stress, plus neurotransmitters like dopamine, serotonin and endorphins.** Dopamine allows you to feel pleasure, satisfaction and motivation. Serotonin is an antidepressant. Endorphins are mild pain relievers. Thus research shows that simply turning up the sides of mouth, even just mechanically, even when you don't feel happy at the moment, can lead to happier feelings after a few minutes. You're hardwired to feel happier when you smile. So, to remain miserable, don't go around smiling like some halfwit, for badness' sake!

Some refer to these as the Happiness Chemicals, and smiling is just one way to stimulate their release in your body. So along with avoiding smiling (you look crazy when you do it anyway!), you'll also want to sidestep, dodge, and circumvent a series of other happiness-inducing actions.

Avoid These Activities That Release Happiness Chemicals:

Dopamine: For Feeling Satisfaction Released when you: • Complete a task • Do self-care • Celebrate wins	**Oxytocin: For Warm Loving Feelings** Released when you: • Play with a baby or pet • Hold hands or hug someone • Give a compliment
Serotonin: For Returning To A Calm State Released when you: • Meditate • Do aerobic exercise • Walk in nature	**Endorphins: For Pain Relief** Released when you: • Laugh • Use essential oils • Eat dark chocolate (You now have an excuse to eat chocolate. You're welcome.)

As you can see, you have many whizbang tools in your Batman Utility Belt of bad moods. Use them frequently and you can maintain and even increase your miserable emotional state. Your bad moods will become as ever-present as that pain-in-the-ass butler Alfred who is always hanging around Batman. You'll need an Alfred-like commitment to serve up hors d'oeuvre of suffering one after another throughout your day. So keep saying "yes please" to those tasty snacks of self-inflicted pain, keep using your bad mood tools like you have been, and stay in your Bat Cave of misery. It's cold, dark, and dank, but it's a familiar place.

NOTES

Write Your Notes Here
(Try not to smear them with your tears. Boo hoo!)

_____

_____

_____

_____

_____

_____

_____

_____

_____

_____

_____

_____

_____

_____

_____

_____

_____

WHEN LIFE GIVES YOU LEMONS, MAKE LEMONADE. THEN THROW IT IN LIFE'S FACE.

Lesson 3:

Interpret Things The Worst Way Possible

Looking on the bright side of life is for creampuffs! Instead, look on the dark side, Darth!

If you're devoted to suffering (and judging from that Resting Miserable Face, you certainly are!), you'll want to bone up on your skills at interpreting all of the events of your life as lacking, awful and simply no good. **Look closer, the awfulness is there. You can find it!**

You can interpret even positive events as negative, it just takes some practice and determination. Your kid got an A on a test. Why not an A+?! You got a raise. Why not more?! You lost 2 lbs. Why not 20?! You get the idea: **there's always a rusty tin lining in any fluffy cloud. Dig in and find it, my miserable apprentice!**

You can even interpret entire eras of your life as awful and no good. **Have you noticed how people are always talking about "these tough times?" Have you also noticed they've talked about tough times in every phase of your life so far?** That's good news for Miserables like you! There's always something going on in the world that makes the current era "tough times." Celebrate that! "Difficult times like this" make even the most committed optimist say "ah fuck it." To be miserable, conclude that today really is the worst of times, believe this is a fact and not an interpretation, embrace that you really are living through hell, deny that things can someday get better, and conclude that life inescapably, invariably is gonna suck now and forever!

To interpret your life the worst way possible, it all starts with expectations: your hopes, dreams, assumptions, and standards about how life should go. The more strangely specific, wildly ambitious and tragically unrealistic your expectations the better. You're a truck driver who wants to be a billionaire-with-a-b? Perfect! You have dreams of being a supermodel even though your face scares the neighbor kids? Now we're talking! You want a huge promotion even though your boss doesn't remember you and calls security when you enter the building? Bingo! Once these expectations are in place, then be completely inflexible about those expectations. Want what you want! Accept nothing else! Expect your life to be not just good but perfect, exactly the way you dreamed it would be! Insist life serve everything you want on a silver platter (preferably from Tiffany's) OR ELSE you will become disappointed and furious. You can do it, Veruca Salt! If you do this, life will never (trust me, never) meet all of your expectations, and so you will be constantly, persistently miserable! "I WANT IT NOW!"

Push out of your mind the fact that your expectations for life are just made-up and YOU made them up! YOU fabricated these expectations about how your life should go. They aren't unquestionably True. These expectations for life are not written in some book in the sky, they're in your noggin (imagine me tapping your head like a hollow pumpkin). You're the expect-er. You're the assessor. You decide to suffer if you're not meeting these expectations. If you're committed to being miserable, then ignore the fact that you made-up how life "should" be, overlook that you made-up the meaning of your current circumstances, and dismiss that you can un-make-up and re-make-up all of this. To remain miserable, derail this new train of thought, throw railroad ties across the tracks quick! To remain miserable, forget you just realized that it's your own internal dialogue that creates expectations, assesses whether or not you're meeting them, and writes the story of your life. Because you create those expectations and you decide how to interpret your circumstances, you determine if your life story is an exciting adventure or feel-good comedy or a pathetic tragedy.

All the stuff that happens in our lives...the neighbor who screams at us, the investments that drop in value, the disease that suddenly shows up...all of it...has no meaning by itself. You can make up either positive or negative stories about stuff like that. You can decide if the neighbor is a no-good so-and-so or someone who needs your kindness. You can decide if your financial picture is doomed or if you can rally to turn it around. You can decide if that disease is the end of joy in life or a valuable reminder to cherish every moment. Because you're committed to being the King of Pain, you know which choice to make. **Decide "life sucks" and oh boy it will!**

Let's talk about the difference between a story and a fact. A fact is an objective reality and has no meaning by itself. A fact is the concrete thing or event, without interpretation or editorial added by you or others. Example: the stock market dropped in value. Conversely, a story is an interpretation, the stuff you make up about the fact, subjective, debatable. Example: The stock market plunged and my entire future is ruined! WAAAAAH! All the meaning is in the story. All the fear is in the story. All the blame is in the story. **All the suffering is in the story, and you wrote the story!** Let the pain begin!

> **Everything you ever wanted is on the other side of fear.**
> **- George Addair**

If there's emotional suffering, an- **guish, depression, guilt, mental up- heaval, and explosive diarrhea, you are the cause (plus maybe that chorizo burrito you had for lunch).**

> **Hide under the covers!**
> **- Me**

The suffering isn't in the facts, the suffering is in the story you made up about the facts.

YOU ARE THE MEANING MAKING MACHINE. BEEP BEEP BOOP!

A dummy falls from a cliff. A human falls from the same cliff. What's the difference between them? The human complains the whole way down. "NO! I DON'T WANT TO DIE! AHHHA!" The dummy doesn't care at all because the dummy can't make up what the fall means. However, you can, my little Meaning Making Machine!

We judge. We interpret. We complain. We make up stories. We add the meaning. Where does the meaning come from? Our words. The words we speak, but also the words we think. You know, that little voice inside your head, the one that's saying, "What little voice inside my head?" That one. **When you observe something, you don't just take it in with your 5 senses, you don't just leave the facts as is. You apply an interpretation, in words, and that creates the meaning of what's happening "out there" in the wild.**

Let's say you're driving down the highway. Suddenly someone

changes lanes and almost hits your car. You could say to yourself, "Oh my gosh, that person is in a hurry! Maybe they're having an emergency. I better get out of their way!" But where's the misery and suffering in that! Instead, scream out loud, "WHAT AN IDIOT! WHAT AN A-HOLE!" That language now defines the event. In fact, in your mind, you didn't just describe the driver as an a-hole, he IS an a-hole. Plus he didn't even give you a "sorry" waive! DOUBLE A-HOLE!

So, if you want to continue to be miserable (looks like you're right on track!), then continue to make up stories full of fairy-tale ideals, wild expectations, dashed hopes, painful exaggerations, emo drama, misinterpretations, leaps in logic, false conclusions, harsh judgements, and whoa-is-me's. Because stories are where suffering lives, where anger is stoked, where the flames of hopelessness are fanned. Dive deep into that pit of despair, you've earned it, you master storyteller you! To continue to be miserable, don't realize that you can change your expectations about life, and make up any story you want about your circumstances. Instead treat these stories as though (here's the cool part) they are not just stories, they are THE TRUTH GOD-DAMMIT! Pretend The Facts and Your Stories are one and the same. And if someone points out another way to interpret something, and presents an alternate story, especially one that's positive and uplifting and hopeful, or if someone simply reminds you of the hard Facts, argue with them! Make sure they know how wrong they are! Tell them that you know a thing or two! And if all else fails, sock 'em in the nose! That'll shut 'em up!

In other words, if you want to continue to be miserable, you'll want to continue to interpret things the worst way possible. But how? It's simple. **Continue this pattern of storytelling that interprets the**

world and your life as awful and no good. You've been doing this with gusto for years, and you can continue for many more!

Whatever you do, never question your stories, reset your expectations, or disturb your interpretations! Never ask yourself questions like:

- "Is this a hard fact or a made-up story?"
- "Is this story helping or hurting me?"
- "What's another interpretation or story I could make up?"
- "What's the happiest, funniest, or most inspiring story I can make up about this?"

Don't do this, my miserable colleague! If you ask questions like these, your mind will search and find answers. And we sure don't want that happening! You might start noticing the difference between Facts and Stories and realize there are countless ways to interpret the world. You just might start choosing to interpret things in a more positive and (guh!) lovely way. And poof there goes the misery!

There are 3 specific types of stories us crazy monkeys make up that really pack a wallop. As you master the art of miserable storytelling, consider using these nifty techniques:

Catastrophizing: This is when you think things are worse than they actually are today, or assume the worst-case scenario will occur in the future. It's distorted thinking and we love all forms of distortion (even that shape of your head over there). Some examples of catastrophizing include:

- If I don't get an A on my final, they'll kick me out of college.
- If I don't finish this report today, I'll be fired.
- This ache probably means I'm dying!

- The stock market went down, and it will never come back up, and I'm going to be homeless in the streets living on crack cocaine and half-empty discarded Red Bulls!

Phew! This can be miserably overwhelming...and that's the point. Whip yourself into a frenzy! Let your thoughts spiral out of control! Blow things out of proportion! Make problems much larger in your mind than they really are! To be miserable, stay in this catastrophic thinking, never reframing your stories and interpretations. Never ask yourself:

- What are the hard facts here vs. my catastrophic story?
- What's another way to look at this situation?
- What positive outcome is even more likely to happen?

Personalizing: This is when you blame yourself for bad things, even when you're not the cause. All the unfortunate stuff that's happening must be your personal fault, right?! HA! What a brilliant way to jump to the wrong conclusion and jump into a big pile of misery! Some specific examples of personalizing include:

- You have a disappointment and assume it's because of some personal flaw (overlooking all the other forces in the world that caused the disappointment).
- Someone else isn't in a good mood, and you blame yourself (overlooking that the other person's own psychology and circumstances largely cause their unhappiness).
- You don't get a promotion at work and assume it's because you aren't good enough (overlooking that the job went to the boss's brother).

- Your friend doesn't call for a week, so you assume she hates you (overlooking that she's going through tough times and needs some solitude).
- You engrave your initials on your new Hermes purse (overlooking that this is an entirely different type of personalizing and is completely off subject. Stay focused!)

To continue being miserable, keep personalizing, making these cognitive distortions and contortions, and assuming you personally are the writer and producer of every shit show in life. Never take steps to see a different perspective. Some specifics actions to avoid:

- Never do a reality check: don't ask yourself if you had control over all of the factors that led to a bad outcome. Don't consider external factors or other people's actions that might have contributed.
- For goodness' sake, don't let go of being responsible for others. Instead, continue to believe that it's up to you to make everyone happy, fulfilled, successful, etc.
- Ignore that disappointment is part of the human experience: Continue overlooking that no one gets everything they want, all the time. Never come to grips with the fact that shit happens, and it happens to everyone, and you only play a small role in the overall shit.

Spotlighting: This is when you overestimate how much others are thinking about or noticing little ol' you. You feel like there is a spotlight on you, revealing your deep flaws and unforgiveable mistakes, for everyone to see. Brightly-lit misery! This bias is common and shows up in every aspect of our lives. For instance:

- You bomb a presentation and feel like everybody must be laughing at you.
- You enter a restaurant and think everyone is harshly judging your outfit.
- You say something incorrect during a group conversation, and someone corrects you. Now everyone knows you're a drooling stupid-head, right?

I hate to break the news to you, but these people probably aren't thinking much about you at all (they're too busy thinking about waffle fries). If you realized nobody is really paying that much attention to you, then you could stop worrying so much about it. Luckily, you haven't mastered the skill of dimming the spotlight yet, and so misery is still yours! To make sure this continues to be the case, never (NEVER!) take action to shine light on the spotlight effect itself. For example:

- Don't consider the fact that no one can read your mind: people often have an "illusion of transparency," believing their internal emotional state and mental thoughts are visible to others. They're not. Us people out here can't read your mind (which is probably a good thing, assuming what you're thinking about over there. Geesh, get your mind out of the gutter!).
- Never focus outward and notice other's actual reactions to you: This would help you to stop focusing inward on your fears, and instead notice how little other people are actually paying attention to you (for instance, I barely remember your name).
- Never ask how you'd react if the roles were reversed: If you find yourself worrying about the kale that was stuck in your teeth at dinner with friends, consider how you'd react if you were

on the other side noticing a friend's kale-encrusted teeth. You probably wouldn't think much of it (maybe you'd just remember to order more floss from Amazon).

As you can see, there are so many ways to interpret things the worst way possible. Continue to ignore hard facts and instead focus on the crazy-ass stories you make up about what's going on in your life. Continue to ignore the fact that these stories are made up, subjective, and open to reevaluation. Continue to forget that you can rewrite your stories to have a more positive interpretation of the past, present and future. Continue to believe your stories and the facts are one and the same. HA! Nice work! Keep doing what you're doing, and misery will be yours in every chapter of your life, my masterful miserable storyteller!

TRUST YOUR GUT.
UNLESS YOUR GUT IS A
NO-GOOD LIAR!

Lesson 4:

Believe Life Has Meaning With A Capital M

Here's an interesting fact for those who want to enjoy a soul-crushing, joy-avoiding, blank-stare-into-the-abyss kind of lifestyle. **Life itself has no meaning whatsoever!** Roll, tears, roll!

If you're a lifetime member of the Misery Club (I saw your membership card in your wallet), you'll want to take advantage of the fact that life is void of meaning by itself. That means you (yes YOU!) get to assign the meaning. You can just make it up! You can decide what life is about. **That's because without you making up what it means, life is inherently about...nothing!** That's beautifully, exquisitely depressing, no?

"How can little ol' me decide the meaning of life?" you ask. "Where can I get a woodfired margherita pizza at this hour?" you continue. I'll focus on answering the first question. All that meaning you think is "out there" isn't out there, it's in your cranium. You made it up. You added the meaning. Meaning is an act of interpretation, of creating a story, about the stuff going on over there beyond the end of your nose.

As noted earlier, YOU are a Meaning Making Machine. An Interpreter Droid. A Story-Writing Robot. Does this compute?

Stuff happens, you notice this, the gears in your head whirl around, the tubes blink on and off, and a slip of paper pops out of your mouth with an interpretation about what that stuff means. Whir, whir, BING! Since it's made up, it is not real, and therefore meaningless. People (including you, buckaroo) assign significance, importance and value to all that stuff out there. But since the meaning is just made up by you, it is meaningless, without substance, and thus changeable, alterable, transformable...by you.

That's why you get to say "LIFE SUCKS!" and it's just as true and valid as anything else coming out of your pie hole like "LIFE IS AN ADVENTURE!" or "LIFE IS INCREDIBLE!" or "LIFE IS A GIFT!" All equally true as your original sucky interpretation.

So, to remain miserable (it's so seductive, no?), simply continue to interpret your life events as awful and no good, shaking your fist at God, the universe, your parents, your in-laws, your neighbors, your boss, the barista, that damn puppy, everyone! You're already doing a great job of making up soul-crushing stories about life (and yourself). Don't interrupt that negative way of thinking, keep it going!

My job is an incredible opportunity. My job is a hell-hole. I'm on my way to success! I'm destined to fail! This pie is good. This pie is bad. It's all made up (except the part about pie, it's always good). So if you're truly, sincerely committed to wallowing in misery (and OH BOY you sure are!) make up some miserable interpretations about life, yourself, others, and baked goods. HATE FREELY!

As human beings, we assign meaning to nearly every experience we have. The meaning we assign is based on our own understanding and life experience to date. Something happens. We don't simply observe what happened, we interpret it, apply words to it, and decide what it means. That's worth saying again. WE DECIDE WHAT IT MEANS. Maybe even again. WE DECIDE WHAT IT MEANS. (I'm tempted to say it a third time, but let's move on). The meaning ain't out there. It's in you.

Here's the super-cool part: **you can pretend like you don't make up the meaning. You can act as though the meaning is fact. You can erroneously conclude your interpretation is THE meaning, the ONLY meaning, amen!** You can pretend your Meaning has a capital M. Solid. Immutable. True for everyone. You know what's what!!

Spoiler alert: If you're going through life with a poor-me victim mentality, like the world has done you wrong, that you can't get a break, that all is lost, that there's no hope, well, sistah, that interpretation of life is all you. You made up it up, it's your made-up story about your life, and if your goal is to be a suffering pile of helplessness, I say good job, mission accomplished!

Spoiler alert part 2: If you feel like you're not good enough and undeserving, that you're not smart enough, not creative enough, not driven enough, not assertive enough, not (fill in the blank) enough to succeed like everybody else on Facebook and TikTok, well, you guessed it, that's not True, that's your story about who you are and what you're capable of, and that story has you playing small, and bumping up against an imaginary lid on your mason jar of life, my little flea.

Spoiler alert part 3: If you feel you're right, really RIGHT, and they're wrong, really WRONG, this is at the heart of conflicts between people. This is what rips families apart. This is where friends transform into enemies. This is at the core of party politics. This is at the center of battles between countries. This is what caused the historical tragedy known as the Cola Wars (neither Coke nor Pepsi won in that carnage). THIS IS WHERE SUFFER-ING IS BORN! I'm RIGHT. You're WRONG. These beautifully hardheaded and thoroughly miserable opposing

Scientists conducted an experiment placing fleas in a glass jar with a lid. The fleas jumped repeatedly in an attempt to escape, but hit the lid and were stopped. Eventually the fleas learned to not jump so high as to hit the lid. In fact, when the lid was removed, they continued to only jump as high as the lid, limiting themselves unnecessarily. Are you like those fleas?

points of view are only possible because we both don't realize we just MADE UP those views. We don't grasp that our own views are often no more true than the other person's views (both likely have truths and fallacies). We each believe we are the keeper of the TRUTH and we'll kill each other (figuratively and literally) for not agreeing with our truth/made-up-shit. "My meaning has a capital M, so treat it with the reverence it deserves goddamnit!"

And if you don't believe every word of this chapter, you're wrong, I'm right, and I'm coming for you, bastard!

EVERYTHING THAT HAPPENS
CAN LEAD TO SOMETHING
GOOD. EXCEPT MEETING
THAT CLOWN IN THE ALLEY.

Lesson 5:

Appreciate Nothing

Eckhart Tolle said, "Acknowledging the good that you already have in your life is the foundation for all abundance." But he's a new-age-y beardo. What does he know?!

Acknowledging the good things in your life leads to feelings of contentment. Satisfaction. Gratitude. But where's the drive in that?! How ya gonna accomplish anything if you feel like what you got is good enough? Instead, foster dissatisfaction! Notice what's missing! **Obsess over the big gaping holes in your life! That'll keep ya looking for more and trying to fill those holes. Fill holes or be one yourself!**

Dear reader, gratitude is for those wimps who want to wallow in mediocrity. It's our perceived lacking in life, the scarcity, the fretting, that drives us and has us striving for more, more, MORE as feverishly as a rat trying to gnaw off its foot stuck in a trap. **Never be satisfied with what ya got! Sure, you'll never feel fulfilled or happy, but big whoop, right?** You'll never learn to be fully present in the now and enjoy the moment. So what?! You'll never put others needs before yours because your own needs will never (NEVER!) be fully met. Who cares (besides everyone in your life)?! That's a small price to pay for having the tenacity and gumption to get the longer job title, the blonder blonde, and the leather seats too!

Let's get down to brass tacks. **Shun the gratitude journal. Never mind mindfulness. Say NO THANKS to thank you's. Don't celebrate...no yippees and for goodness' sake no yahoos.** Grace shouldn't be said before a meal unless that's the waitress's name and she's late with your cup of joe!

Don't look at the good. Overlook it. Deny it. What good?

Don't see life as a gift. See it as a given. Like it's owed to you.

Appreciate no one, including yourself. You, and they, could be so much more perfect-er!

In your moments of disappointment, don't consciously shift your mental focus toward things you're grateful for. Don't ask yourself what's great in your life. Don't put reminders of who or what you love on your mirror to see each morning. You can focus on anything you want, good or bad, so focus on what's not there, what's missing, what's lost, what you must have but can't. **Sure, you could focus on the sweet kitten rubbing your leg, but dammit you wanted a dog!**

Don't ask sappy questions like, "What am I grateful for?" Or "Who do I love?" Or "What was a blessing in my life, even if now gone?" Because, guess what, your brain will search around and find answers. You don't want

EYE-ROLLING QUOTE OF THE DAY:

"What is grief, if not love persevering?"
- Vision, *WandaVision*

answers. They will cause you to miss what's missing in your life. As you seek, so shall you find. So don't seek what you're grateful for or you'll find it, and then you'll feel (grr) content.

Some namby-pamby people believe that when we practice gratitude and remind ourselves what is already good in our life, we draw more good to us. Puh-leeze! The theory is, by thinking about what we're thankful for, and bringing our mental focus toward the things we love and cherish, our mind then, consciously and unconsciously, seeks and finds more of these good things. In this way, we supposedly can "manifest" more good in our life. Yeah, simply by focusing on and being grateful for what we already have we can create more. But I say, come down off of that cloud! **If simply appreciating what's good could make more good, then Mother Teresa would have owned a mega-yacht. (No need to Google it. She didn't.)** SO WHAT if she was grateful for her life, appreciated what little she had, focused on serving others, felt one with God, was loved by millions, lived a life of deep purpose and meaning, and died an international hero. No yacht, no happy, that's my motto.

Some begin their day with gratitude questions, asking themselves "What am I grateful for? Who do I love? What do I appreciate?" I say quit focusing on what you already got, you already got it! Instead, focus on what you don't got, why you don't got it, and how ya gonna get it! Then work frantically and spastically to get that stuff!

Sure, **Harvard Medical School concluded that gratitude is consistently associated with greater happiness,** positive emotions, improved health, ability to deal with adversity, and stronger relationships. Similarly, **UC Davis psychologist Robert Emmons found that keeping a gratitude journal—regularly writing brief re-**

flections on moments we're thankful for—can significantly increase feelings of well-being and life satisfaction. But what do all those highfalutin research-y people know?! We don't have time to read research! We've got a hamster wheel to run on! What I'm desperately trying to say to you is, foster anti-gratitude! Ignore the mountain of evidence that shows the real-world benefits of cultivating appreciation. Snub the fact that, **according to Psychology Today, there are 7 scientifically proven benefits of gratitude:**

1. Gratitude opens the door to more relationships.
2. Gratitude improves physical health.
3. Gratitude improves psychological health.
4. Gratitude enhances empathy and reduces aggression.
5. Gratitude helps you sleep better.
6. Gratitude improves self-esteem.
7. Gratitude increases mental strength.

Gratitude, gratitude, gratitude! What do psychologists today (or any day) really know!? We're not here to be all science-y. We're here to be Ungrateful, Needy, Desperate and Miserable! In fact, let's be grateful we're NOT grateful!

How do you stamp out gratitude in yourself, you may ask? Oh, I've got an assignment for you!

The 7-Day Anti-Gratitude Challenge:

To help you make misery a lifestyle, here's my 7-Day Anti-Gratitude Challenge! Are you willing to take this on for a week? **Don't worry, this challenge is as easy as taking a rattle from a baby, and as misery-inducing as being hit in the face with a cat**—all designed to encourage you to throw gratitude to the wind. And, chances are, you're already doing most of this, my miserable compadre! Don't stop now!

Day 1: Make A List Of What You Don't Appreciate.

On the first day of your Journey to Anti-Gratitude, create a list of 10 things, big or small, that you resent in your life. (This should be easy, since you've been doing this in your head your whole life, right?!) **Ask: what do you begrudge? What in your life is no bueno?** Once you have your list, spend some quality time thinking about these gaping wounds in your life. Obsess about your problems. Examine your failings. Micro-analyze life's imperfections. Let your pain fester. Bonus assignment: share your list of resentments with family and friends (because misery sure does love company).

Day 2: Find Fault In Your Body

Your body is your temple...your broken-down, lopsided, ghetto temple. Spend some time today noticing all the imperfections and health issues you have (you're already skilled with this, no?). That mole. Those extra pounds. Those sweaty hands. That trick knee. Make a list (mental or written) and share your Body of Evidence (get it?) with your family and friends. Make sure they know you're fully aware your body has failed you miserably, and you're nothing more than a walking, talking pile of goo.

Ignore the fact that in this galaxy swirling with seemingly random atoms and molecules, the fact that you exist — that any life exists — is an improbability and thus an absolute miracle. Ignore that beyond any likelihood, dumb matter became life, then became conscious, then evolved to the point of thinking, understanding, loving, striving and creating. Sure, this realization can take your breath away as you stare into the face of God/ the Universe/Karma. But this is all just a distraction. Discipline. Forget about the miracle you are and instead ask, "Why do I have this muffin top!?"

Day 3: Spend Time Today Judging Others

Your family and friends. They are such a blessing. Still, throw them under the bus! **Today, dig and uncover all that's wrong with the people in your life.** How they never call. That shirt. The way they chew. UGH! Ignore the good times. Focus on the irritants. Think about all that you HATE about the people you love. Admit it, you already do this, just do more of it! And if you're truly committed to an f-ed up life, share your list of complaints with the offender – it will be like throwing a grenade into the relationship. KA-BOOM BABY! Chunks of misery everywhere!

Day 4: Treat Those Who Serve You Like Vending Machines

Cashiers, baristas, waitresses, doormen. They're not people, they're randos. Treat them as such. They are only there to serve YOU.

Don't take the time to look them in the eye and really thank them. They're getting paid, aren't they? Do your job, people!

Don't treat these strangers like equals. Don't offer them kindness or consideration. Earn an A+ at being an A-hole. Hand over your credit card without even looking up from your phone. Sure, it only takes two seconds to look at them, make eye contact, connect, smile, thank them, and perhaps make their day. But why would you want to be the person who restores their faith in humanity? They need to get you that Venti Macchiato pronto, dammit?!

Grow those feelings of entitlement. Foster grumpiness toward strangers. Greenlight that low-level anger toward others. If you're doing it right, at least a few times a week, you should be causing some tears over there with these strangers, whether you see them cry live in person (always fun), or the tears role later when they are home and remembering your mean-spirited interaction. It takes some faith to know the tears are rolling behind closed doors. Believe!

Day 5: Thank No One.

Today, practice ignoring those who help you. **Undoubtedly people in your present and past contributed to you in some way. They provided help, encouragement, coaching, assistance, money, a job, a big break, a sympathetic ear, a sympathetic nose, whatever, and this set your life in a new direction.** Remember when you had that big breakup and your friend comforted you? Remember when you couldn't make rent and mom and dad footed the bill? Remember when you tried to drink your own weight in Jägermeister and your friend took away the 9th bottle? Those moments likely changed the trajectory of your life. This new direction is what caused you to reach your destiny today. The "you" that you refer to today wouldn't have happened without assistance from those around you.

Okay, they made a difference in your life, big whoop, right?! You don't want to admit that, do you? **To admit that someone else contributed to who you are today is like admitting you have some lack, that you couldn't have done it without them. Don't admit that!** You are a rock. You are an island. You are whole and complete without anyone else's help. Thanking others for what they've done for you is like admitting you're incomplete by yourself, acknowledging you're interconnected with others, that "You" is partly dependent on "Them." Bull. Thank no one. You are Self-Made! Your success lies within YOU, not with those outsiders. You don't need to clink glasses with anyone. Raise your glass to yourself!

Day 6: Start Your Morning Anticipating A Painful Day

This morning your assignment is to spend time dreading the day ahead. (If you already do this, way to go, you miserable teacher's pet!). **Think about all that can go wrong today. Focus on the unpleasantness that can come your way. Then...make it come true. Self-fulling prophecies!** That meeting later today? You just KNOW you're going to do horribly. That lunch date? You just KNOW he's going to be a no-show. Going to finally try that new workout? You just KNOW you're gonna pull a muscle. When you look into the future, and predict problems and pain, two wonderful things happen: you suffer now as you envision that miserable broken-ass future, plus you make it more likely that your horrific vision will become real (your mind is amazingly effective at making what it imagines into reality). So start a morning ritual of imagining and predicting the Worst Day Ever and, by cracky, you're likely to suffer your way to making it real!

Day 7: End Your Day Remembering What Went Wrong

As you tuck yourself into bed tonight for a long winter's (or whatever fricking season's) nap, ask yourself: what was a shitshow today? What didn't you get done today? Who wronged you today? **It's not enough to have experienced troubles in the moments throughout your day. You must remember those headaches, and reexperience them over and over again. You know, like you've been doing your entire life, right?!** Keep a mental scrapbook of your pain. Keep those painful memories alive. Rub salt in those wounds by reminding yourself of your mistakes and defeats. Remember how you asked that girl out and she laughed so hard Topo Chico came out her nose. Bitch! Remember walking up to the podium in front of all those people and tripping on perfectly flat carpet. What's wrong with you?! Remember that workout you were supposed to do but you had half a jar of cookie butter instead. Loser! Picture again that waiter who forgot to leave tomatoes off your salad. Bastard! Bring them all to mind as you try to drift off to sleep. It was a bad day. Remember it. Dream about it. And be ready for another doozy tomorrow.

Once you complete the 7-Day Anti-Gratitude Challenge, the good news is, you never have to end it! You can live this challenge over and over again like you're Bill Murray in *Groundhog Day*. So spend today...and tomorrow...and the next day...fostering anti-gratitude, and digging a happiness-shaped hole in your heart. This will drive you wonderfully mad as you frantically try to fill that hole with something. Anything. Maybe cake!

NOTES

Write Your Notes Here
(Could be new profound insights. Or your grocery list. Whatev.)

GRAB LIFE BY THE COJONES!
UNLESS YOU DON'T WANT
A HANDFUL OF COJONES.

Lesson 6:

Learn To Be Helpless

I n order to stick to your Misery Pledge (and I see your right hand up), another neat-o skill to develop is something called Learned Helplessness.

Now don't get me wrong, we want to avoid learning in most instances. But here's an exception worth making. **Learned Helplessness occurs when someone continuously faces a negative situation and eventually stops trying to change circumstances, even when the person has the ability to do so.** Bingo-bango-bongo! The person gives up! Misery is produced!

Learned Helplessness is a kind of "fake conclusion" where we infer that there is nothing we can do to improve a situation. **This fake conclusion is perfect for those who want to sleep on a proverbial bed of nails all life long! Zzzz...ouchy!**

Learned Helplessness is universal and has been observed even in animals. Martin Seligman (okay, I'll admit I have no idea who he is either) first observed Learned Helplessness when he was doing experiments on dogs. He noticed that the dogs didn't try to escape electric shocks if they had been conditioned to believe they couldn't. In other sad puppy news: domestic dogs have demonstrated Learned Helplessness when they believe they have no choices in their circumstance. For example, dogs in puppy farms, who often experience little kindness, can act helpless even after being placed in a kind home. Dogs are just the beginning. **Research has observed Learned Helplessness in basically all animals.**

Spoiler alert: humans are animals.

Spoiler alert #2: you're a human.

If you're committed to living an unfulfilled and miserable life, like no-kidding really committed, then Learned Helplessness is a whiz-bang tool you can use in nearly any situation or circumstance! Relationships, jobs, health, that hair style (geesh), anything! Simply surrender. Tap out! Say uncle!

Let's say you're in a loveless relationship. Maybe even abusive. You've been treated with indifference or meanness for quite some time. The door is right there. You could bolster your courage and walk out, taking back your life triumphantly. But you don't leave. That's Learned Helplessness, my well-conditioned friend. You've been trained to stay. Good girl!

Let's say you're in a job where you aren't appreciated or rewarded. You probably live in a country that allows you to choose whatever job you want (unless you're a commie). Yet you stay in that mind-numbing, soul-sucking dull-as-dishwater job year after year. That's Learned Helplessness. Stay...stay...okay here's a treat!

People often justify Learned Helplessness with an explanatory narrative – a story to rationalize why taking action won't work, like, "I'd change jobs except this job pays my bills and what if I took a new job and it didn't work out and I was fired and then I'd have no paycheck and couldn't make rent and my landlord kicked me out of my apartment then I became homeless and while homeless became addicted to crack cocaine and then OD'ed and died so obviously I can't change jobs because I don't want to be a crack whore and die!" And thus the shackles get a little tighter.

All of our lives are peppered with instances of Learned Helplessness. Some big. Some small. We overlook how we have influence in all situations (except who will get a rose on *The Bachelor*: I have a conspiracy theory on how THAT'S determined!). We are never truly helpless, there's always an action we can take. But to stay miserable, shut those thoughts down! Pull the curtains closed on that ray of hope! **Believe (falsely) you can't change your circumstance. Stay where you are, you lazy old dog, and lap up that big bowl of misery! Woof!**

How will you know you finally have the ultimate squeaky toy called Learned Helplessness in your paws? Look for these signs:

5 Signs of Learned Helplessness

- **Low self-esteem:** you believe YOU are the problem.
- **Frustration:** you believe there's no way to get what you want.
- **Passivity:** you accept what's happening without resistance.
- **Lack of effort:** why bother, right?
- **Giving up:** you take some action, don't get the result immediately, so you stop.

My sister lived a life of Learned Helplessness. She was all-in on her helplessness, committed to playing small, and eager to delegate handling her troubles to others in her life – family, friends, even strangers. She believed she had little ability to handle life's challenges, and by believing this, it became true. She stayed in a job that she hated for years, never having the courage to try something different. She dated loser boyfriends over and over again until they ironically left her. She put up with being overweight and unhealthy for years, eventually leading to diabetes, which lead to kidney failure, and years on dialysis (there's no better way to spend a Saturday than hooked up to a machine, right!?). The doctors advised her that through physical exercise and good nutrition, this situation was manageable, possibly even reversable. Yet my committedly-helpless sister did nothing to help herself. She didn't lift a finger, in fact, she didn't lift a leg. That's because it became harder to walk, so she decided to never go anywhere that had a curb or a step, to avoid having to lift her legs up that small distance. (Spoiler alert: nearly all places have curbs or steps.) If you think Learned Helpless is a cakewalk, a ticket to the easy life, oh I beg to differ. The sandbox my sister played in became smaller and smaller over time. She was miserable, and you can be too by simply mastering Learned Helplessness.

Some Students of Misery (maybe you included) may need to be hit over the head with the obvious in order to master Learned Helplessness. So, **let me point out WHY you (like my sister) might use Learned Helplessness, even if unconsciously: it's because along with the COSTS, there are big-time, seductive BENEFITS.**

What does it COST you to believe you're helpless?	How does it BENEFIT you to believe you're helpless?
• Self-expression • Freedom • Passion • Respect (from others and yourself) • Success • Fulfillment • A life you love! • $13.99 (tax not included)	• You can avoid failure • Put in less effort • Get others to do stuff for you • Dodge taking risks • Remain in the familiar • Receive sympathy from others • Get love and attention too (poor thing!) • Avoid taking responsibility for your life • People may bring over casseroles (and who doesn't like casseroles?!)

So, to be as miserable as possible, continue to pursue the creepy benefits of Learned Helplessness, no matter how small that has you playing in life, no matter how pathetic a life it creates. Continue to ignore the high costs of Learned Helplessness, and never realize these gigantic costs far outweigh the unsatisfying benefits. These costs may eventually include everything you care about – relationships, success, health, even your life, like it did for my sister. **Sometimes the smallest step in the right direction ends up being the biggest step you can take. But to remain miserable, keep believing you aren't able to take that small step. Keep believing the curbs and steps of life are insurmountable obstacles, and they will be.**

NOTES

Draw Your Vision Of Your Future Here
(Probably a nightmarish hellscape if I know you!)

Lesson 7:

You're Da Man, So Go It Alone

Whether you're Da Man, or Da Woman, you're a "Da". So you don't have to listen to anyone.

You came into this world alone, and you should go through it that way, you lone wolf you! Quit reaching out for help from people who could teach you, uplift you, assist you, inspire you, or hold your hoop earrings while you cat fight! Success with help from others is not success at all, right?! Quit being so needy! Quit sharing the glory! Quit being a wuss!

Sure, misery loves company. But misery doesn't want anyone's goddamn help!

Who are these people to tell you what to think or do, right? Learn from no one. You're complete and whole the way you are. You can do anything you need to on your own (except put together that Ikea NORDLI bed...even I'll admit absolutely no one can do that without help). Grow? There's nowhere to grow, you're already 100%! Consider another perspective? Um, no, if another person is right, you must be wrong, never admit that! Emulate someone who achieved what you want? Don't take short cuts, sissy! Sure, success leaves clues...for the clueless. Find your own path in life even if you gotta hack through the dense brush and endure some snakebites!

Letting others contribute to you, and learning from them, is like admitting you are incomplete or lacking. The hell with that! You went through grade school, probably high school too (well la-di-dah!). That should be enough learning and growing, thank you!

They say we can stand on the shoulders of giants. But we can also fall from way up there and smack our head against the ground! Why risk it? Sure, leveraging the experience and wisdom of others who have gone before us can help us make progress way quicker and easier. Yeah, we can uncover new truths by examining previous discoveries. Of course, if we stand on the shoulders of giants we can see farther. But those giants might start walking in a direction we don't want to go, with us going along for the ride, flailing around up on their shoulders. We'll have none of that! We are self-directed, eye-on-the-prize, you-go-your-way-I'll-go-mine guys and gals, right? SO WHAT if it takes us 10 times as long to go the same distance, or maybe never even get to our desired destination. We're not getting help. We're not shoulder-riders!

That means we really have no need to learn from thought leaders, intellectuals, sages, gurus, and people who know things we don't of any type. Who are they to tell us what to think or do?

- Fuck others.
- Fuck facts.
- Fuck teachers.
- Fuck scientists.
- Fuck the educated.
- Fuck the successful.
- Fuck the experienced.
- Fuck different perspectives.
- Fuck your elders (Grammy too!).
- Fuck Oprah (yeah, I said it!).
- Fuck me too.

Those who want success quicker and easier don't go it alone (wimps). They find someone who has achieved the same goal and emulate the steps they took to reach their outcome. This is a speedier (and wussier) way to achieve results. It shortens the learning curve to anything they want to master. It's like following someone's easy peasy recipe to produce a Bundt cake of success. Those who want an easier (and spineless) path to success can follow these Life Hacks (but YOU better not or I'll tear this book out of your frail pathetic hands!):

Wimpy Life Hacks To Get Success:

Wimpy Life Hack #1: Whatever you want to achieve, someone has already done it. Find that person. Such a person can save you immense amounts of time and pain. Leverage their knowledge and experience.

Wimpy Life Hack #2: Model that person who has already succeeded at what you're trying to accomplish. Don't reinvent the wheel. Want to make horseshoes (who doesn't)? Learn from a blacksmith and do what he does.

Wimpy Life Hack #3: Copy their strategy. Those who succeed consistently aren't just lucky, they're taking actions that others aren't. By copying their strategy and actions, you'll be able to achieve similar results, and faster. Like decades faster. It doesn't matter what you're trying to do — whether you want to be a writer (you fool!) or an entrepreneur or a bodybuilder, someone's already done it splendidly and their blueprint can be followed.

Wimpy Life Hack #4: Instead of modeling what successful people are doing now, model what they did BEFORE they were successful. Copy the strategy and actions they used BEFORE they produced the result, not after. Those early steps are what took them to success.

Wimpy Life Hack #5: Get over the idea that you're stealing from others. That's not what we're talking about. There's a difference between copyright infringement (this leads to jailtime with a woman who smells like cigarettes and cheese) and following in the footsteps of someone who achieved the result you want (this leads to you sitting in a bathtub full of money like Scrooge McDuck). Don't plagiarize copyrighted material. Don't steal a patent. Instead, seek inspiration from others. Copy their path, their steps, their mindset, but not their material.

Now that you're learned those Wimpy Life Hacks, shake 'em off. That section was only a cautionary tale, how the wimpy succeed, intended for only the most hacky of life hackers, and that ain't you, right?!

You are an island. And an island never emulates.

Instead, remember that learning from others and following their steps to success might produce the results you want in life, sure, but only because some goody two-shoes helped your weak ass. **Only babies need help (those pathetic lumps!). Go it alone. You are Da Man or Da Woman but not Da Baby!**

Carve your own path in life. So what if there's a nice clear path someone else created right in front of your peepers and you can simply follow it? Instead, ignore it, look the other way, dive into the thick of the jungle, and struggle and toil to clear your own twisted gnarled path one hard-fought inch at a time. Keep hacking with that machete! Get that beetle off your back! Don't Life Hack, instead hack your own path, and you can become a hack yourself!

WHO CAN ACHIEVE ANYTHING? WHO CAN SOLVE ANY PROBLEM? WHO'S BIG ENOUGH TO HANDLE ANY CHALLENGE?

TURN THE PAGE TO FIND OUT.

NOT YOU
HAHAHA

This was supposed to be an actual shiny mirror right inside the book. But I didn't have the budget. Get off my back!

←

Lesson 8:

Ask Bad Questions

You're a member of the secret society of the Miserati, right? Well, you got your lifetime membership in part by asking misery-inducing questions. "Why would I ask misery-inducing questions? You think I'm some sort of moron?" Yeah, questions like that. **By asking miserable questions, you get miserable answers, and anguish is born!** Here's your membership card.

We all have a dialogue going on in our head. A little voice that's always talking to us, giving a play-by-play commentary on all that's happening around us. A large part of that inner dialogue is made up of questions. We ask ourselves questions all day long. "What questions?" There's one. And our brain searches around and finds answers to those questions.

Let's say you ask positive questions like "How can I make this a great day?" Your brain will come up with answers, and off you go on your nauseatingly happy and excruciatingly sunshiny day. On the other hand, **let's say you ask yourself questions like "Why does everyone have it better than me?" Your brain will answer that question as well and come up with reasons others have it better than you. Like, you're a talentless schmuck. Nice work!** As you can see, we can either ask life-affirming questions or misery-inducing questions. Choose the latter, my cheerless friend. MINIACLE LAUGH!

Lost? Confused? A little slow? Here are some tips on asking the right types of wrong questions, and the wrong types of right questions.

First, ask open-ended questions instead of closed-ended. "What's the difference?" you ask. Good question, you question-generating machine! Open-ended questions allow you to give a free-form answer... anything that comes to mind. Closed-ended questions are answered abruptly with "yes or no" or "this or that." **Closed-ended questions are less engaging because they are answered quickly and definitively. Open-ended questions are more engaging because they encourage your mind to explore, think of options, debate on the answer, and stop daydreaming about stuffed crust pizza for a few moments.**

Another tip: avoid heaping questions, one on top of another. That's a big no-no. When you ask questions one after another, it confuses your puny human brain. You won't know which question to answer. You'll overload the circuits in your Meaning Making Machine. Beep beep BOOM! Instead, ask one question at a time, and pause. Let your brain spit out an answer.

Jennifer Coolidge in the movie *Best in Show* knows the value of listening to that inner voice, one message at a time. She says, "I feel that I really need to listen to my inner instinct. And my inner instinct says don't go right now. So I'm not going. I'm going to be right here until I get another message...from myself." Excellent job, Jennifer Coolidge. Listen to that inner voice one message at a time.

We're all like snot-nosed kids who love to ask questions. We love to talk to ourselves about ourselves, plus ask questions about everything that parades in front of our peepers. So learn to do it the right way. **Master the art of asking questions that keep you nicely, firmly miserable. Interrogate yourself like a captured terrorist! Inquire yourself into the abyss! Turn that smile upside down with awful questions!**

"What questions should I ask?" I suggest asking yourself the right (well, left) questions in the chart.

(This area left blank because
we're lazy typographers.)

To be miserable, ask these questions:	To be a happy (sigh), ask these questions:
Why does my life suck?	What's good in my life right now?
What's wrong with me?	What's my superpower?
Why does this shit always happen to me?	What can I learn from this?
How can I look good and not be discovered as a fraud?	How can I make a difference here?
Who the hell does he think he is?	What can this person teach me?
Why can't I get what I want?	What steps can I take to get what I want?
Why is this so hard?	How can I enjoy the process and make it fun?
Why can't I make this work?	How can I cause a breakthrough?

Start and End Your Day with Miserable Questions

Consider starting each morning with questions that set a miserable tone to your upcoming day. Then at the end of the day, review the lousy stuff that happened to make sure you remember all of that pain!

You can do this in your head, or even better, write it on paper or digital screen. Do I mean a smarmy "Gratitude Journal"? Um, thankfully no. Instead, **I suggest you keep a Misery Journal to keep track of all that's wrong with your life (you've been doing this casually for years, now let's formalize it!).** Make sure you have plenty of pages, you'll need 'em!

More specifically (because you're a little vacant), start every day by asking yourself awful, no-good questions. Here are some examples (maybe you already ask yourself some of these!):

- **What crap do I have to do today?**
- **How am I going to get all that shit done?**
- **How can I avoid that meeting I'm dreading?**
- **Why do I have to deal with that jerk at work?**
- **How can I get back at so-and-so?**
- **Why does my life suck so hard?**
- **Why can't I find time for the things I like to do?**
- **Is it the weekend yet?**

Ask yourself questions like these at the start of your day (judging from that scowl, you already do!) and VIOLA! You'll be as miserable as a cartoon character with an anvil dropped on his head. **Whatever you do, don't let positive questions drift into your noggin at the start of your day – questions like:**

- **What's going to be fun today?**
- **What can I learn today?**
- **How can I make a difference today?**
- **What can make today an adventure?**

- **What will make this a day to remember?**
- **How can I move my goals forward today?**
- **How can I kick that problem's ass today?**

If you ask questions like these at the start of your day, you might end up having a happy, beautiful, fully-present day. And we'll have none of that!

The start of your day is just half of the equation. The end of your day is another opportunity to torture yourself and tighten the wheels of the mental rack you're stretched out on. Youch! **To drift off to sleep in misery, and dream of the dreaded all night long, end your day by asking yourself awful, no-good questions like these (sound familiar?):**

- **Why did today suck so bad?**
- **How could I embarrass myself like that?**
- **What the hell was I thinking?**
- **Why is my boss always busting my balls?**
- **Why did I get married?**
- **Why did I have kids?**
- **How do I get revenge on so-and-so?**
- **Can I just stay in bed tomorrow?**

Don't let positive questions like these enter your thoughts as you drift off to sleep:
- **What was great today?**
- **What did I learn today?**
- **How did I make a difference today?**

- **What was fun today?**
- **What did I accomplish?**
- **Who did I love today?**
- **Who loved me today?**
- **What made me feel alive today?**

Let's face it, all of this is nothing new to you. You've been asking and answering miserable questions every day since you were young. So think of this as a refresher, just reaffirming that your lifelong habits and techniques are spot on for creating a Terrible, Horrible, No Good, Very Bad Day. Keep it up, Alexander! Why change now when you're on a roll!

Your questions control your focus, and your focus becomes your experience of life. Choose your questions wisely. If you ask miserable questions, you will come up with miserable answers — and therefore a miserable life. And that's nothing to question, is it?

NOTES

Write Your Notes Here
(For fun, use your left hand so it looks like a ransome note!)

_____

_____

_____

_____

_____

_____

_____

_____

_____

_____

_____

_____

_____

_____

_____

_____

_____

_____

Lesson 9:

Take, Don't Give

Misery loves company, and it looks like you're having a raging party over there! How did so many people get so miserable? Like you, they've gotten into the habit of taking, not giving. **Nothing can pack a misery party like a good ol' take-don't-give, me-focused, what's-mine-is-mine-and-what's-yours-is-mine attitude.** It's like lapping up body shots off the flabby abs of Satan himself.

Sadly, pathetically, us humans have an innate urge to make a difference. It's programmed into us. The wusses and the weak want to help, give, contribute, make the world a better place, and make others smile. Ick. Resist that urge. Stuff those feelings down hard like a day old chimichanga with no horchata chaser. **Humans naturally, instinctively, and sadly have a need for service: we have this desire to help, give and support others.** It's a desire as burning as untreated jock itch. This burning desire can come in many forms, like the desire to work in a soup kitchen for the homeless, sure, but the desire to contribute can come in subtler forms, like leading at work, serving in the military, and mentoring a no-good undeserving stink-infused child. We've all heard others say, "I want to make a difference." And we've all responded by rolling our eyes so hard we pulled an ocular muscle. That's because you and I, dear reader, are different. We are ready to deny our instinctual need to give back, push down our inborn desire to help others, put off volunteering until "someday," and turn our backs on the very thing that would fulfill us the most! Guillermo, pour us another misery shot! Andale, andale!

Why should you avoid giving and contributing? There are so many reasons. First, making a difference takes effort. We don't do effort. Second, helping

A QUOTE AS DUMB AS IT IS LONG:

This is the true joy in life, the being used for a purpose recognized by yourself as a mighty one; the being a force of nature instead of a feverish, selfish little clod of ailments and grievances complaining that the world will not devote itself to making you happy.

I am of the opinion that my life belongs to the whole community, and as long as I live it is my privilege to do for it whatever I can.

I want to be thoroughly used up when I die, for the harder I work the more I live. I rejoice in life for its own sake. Life is no "brief candle" for me. It is a sort of splendid torch which I have got hold of for the moment, and I want to make it burn as brightly as possible before handing it on to future generations.

- George Bernard Shaw

others causes us to think beyond ourselves, and be "over there" in others' worlds, rather than squarely focused on our own wants and needs. Sorry, we need to stay focused on Numero Uno! Third, contributing to others will inevitably have you asking icky questions like "What's my purpose in life? Is there something bigger than myself? Is 'me vs. you' an illusion? Are we all actually One?" Shake it off, Taylor Swift!

Besides, who are you to make a difference? The list of problems that our society is facing is daunting and overwhelming. So why bother? Just pour some Velveeta over those nachos and call it a day! Someone else will fix things, right?

Plus, even if we did want to change the world, we'd want to do it quick, like in a day, not weeks, months, or years! Some problems are small and swiftly managed, but some problems are big and take ginormous amounts of time to solve, with a slow steady effort. Who has the time and stamina for that? Sure, you and I will likely be on this planet for years more, and we could use those years to make the world a better place. **But I have a hard time keeping up with groceries each week, let alone making plans for a world-changing project that might take years to accomplish. That would take knowing how I want to make a difference long-term, breaking it down into steps, consistently taking action, chipping away and making progress one step at a time.** Easy peasy, sure, but most people don't seem to know this so shhhh don't you say a word!

As you can see, **there are so many things that can trip you up when trying to give back and make a difference in the world. Finding time is one stumbling block (and you love to go headlong over that one, don't you?!).** Another stumbling block is lack of skills and resources to accomplish the change you want. Overlook that others have those skills and resources you lack, and you can simply ask for their help. Tapping others is a no-no: you don't want others to think you are lacking in any way, do you? Ask for no help. Use no one else's knowledge or skills. Muddle along on your own, like a dung beetle pushing along its ball of poo.

I sense you're starting to understand this core misery-inducing idea: It's better to take than to give. However, one word of caution. It's a mine field of opportunities to contribute out there! There are so many ways to give back to society and make a difference with others. From big ways to small ways. Here are just some you want to watch out for, and step over carefully like a landmine.

How To Take, Not Give, And Thus Remain Miserable:

DON'T make life better for anyone else! Supporting your spouse, encouraging your children, helping your parents, being there for your friends – they are all ways to contribute, and they all should be avoided! You don't want all these people thinking you're going to do stuff for them all the time, do you? You'll get busy with that stuff and miss some good binge watching!

DON'T mentor anyone! Teaching someone younger or less experienced than you is a way to make a difference. This can include mentoring someone at work, at a local school, at a special-interest club, in an elevator (you gotta be quick!), or whatever. Pay it forward? NO, BACK THAT UP! The person you mentor is going start asking questions, lots of questions, and this grilling is going to lead to you being discovered as a fraud, a fake, a no-nothing loser! Who are you to help? What the heck do YOU know? (Now you're using your misery-inducing questions from Lesson 8. Nice work!) Let me mentor you on just one thing: to remain miserable like you want, mentor no one!

DON'T treat others with kindness! Being kind to others is a way to contribute to them. This often requires forgetting about ourselves for awhile and instead thinking about the other person's feelings. But WHO CARES about other people's feelings!? Sure, a small act of kindness can make someone's day. Opening a door for someone. Allowing someone to go in front of us in line. Letting someone take the last piece of bread. Wrestling a bear while a family escapes. These small gestures can make someone believe in humanity again. But we all know that humanity is not worth believing in, so stop misleading people with your good deeds!

DON'T give your true self to the world! They say (whoever they are) that you can contribute to the world simply by being your true, authentic self. Just by being you, you can make a difference. "They" continue that we each have a unique perspective, individual insights and distinct talents to share. No one is quite like you. I say thank goodness there's no one else like you, because one of you is plenty! Hide your true self, cover that shit up (especially that mole on your face) and pretend to be someone you're not. You've always believed you're not good enough. I say you were right! So reject your true self, put on a mask, and act like someone else, someone better. Sure, denying your true self can lead to a soul-crushing inauthenticity, a lifeless, joyless existence. But as Billy Crystal said, "It's better to look good than to feel good." And you look marvelous...when you're pretending to be someone you're not! So give the world the gift of not-you, and suffer on, my miserable two-faced friend!

DON'T volunteer! An all-too-common way to give back to the world is volunteering. They say (there "they" go again) that finding a cause that you believe in and helping with that effort can lead to a life of purpose and feeling like your life matters. However, I strongly assert that a life of purpose is overrated!

A study from the London School of Economics examined the relationship between volunteering and happiness (I guess they got tired of studying economics!) **The researchers found that the more people volunteered, the happier they were.** For example, compared with people who never volunteered, the odds of being "very happy" rose 12% for those who volunteered just every 2-4 weeks. Well, I say, shut your scone hole, London School of Economics, we're too busy to volunteer and be "very happy"!

Volunteering is only for those who have nothing better to do, right? You've got the next level to get to in Super Mario! You've got nails that aren't going to gel themselves!

So ignore and deny that volunteering:

- Gives you a sense of purpose
- Helps you forget your own problems
- Connects you with others
- Builds self-esteem
- Increases your social skills
- Contributes to your mental health
- Provides networking for your career
- Plus you probably can sneak a bowl of soup for yourself

DON'T try to save the planet! Some people believe in science and all that climate change mumbo jumbo. Not us, right?! We're smarter than that! The planet is so big, and you're so small. How could you (or 8 billion of you) negatively affect the environment? SO WHAT that every reputable scientist is in agreement that climate change is real, happening now, and we gotta act fast in order to save the panda's ass as well as our own. Shut your carbon-neutral mouth! We're just trying to get to the weekend! Don't give back to Mother Earth. Take what she owes you! Suck up all the resources on the planet and leave a wake of non-biodegradable plastic. **There are so many ways you can take from our planet. Use lots of plastic (especially bottled water because tap is for wusses, right?!). Avoid recycling (landfills the size of a mountain are kinda cool, don't ya think?!). Keep guzzling gas and keep shoveling coal (so climate change can transform Cleveland into a tropical winter getaway!)**

Those are just some of the ways you can take, not give. Don't take all of this taking for granted. Work on your taking skills every day, like you have since birth, you selfish miserable beastie! You've gotten better and better at taking over the years. Keep it up! Snub that burning desire to make the world a better place. Ignore the instinct to give back. Turn your back on your innate need to contribute to others. Avoid looking at this uncomfortable and ironic truth that will spin your head around: by giving we have more, by taking we have less.

NOTES

**Take Notes Like A T-Rex
(Use shorthand)**

THEY SAY YOU MISS 100%
OF THE SHOTS YOU DON'T
TAKE. BUT THEY AREN'T
GOOD AT MATH.

Lesson 10:

Focus On Trivial Shit

Want to continue to be miserable? (You must if you've read all the way to this chapter!) **Keep focusing on all the trivial stuff in your life, and let it distract you from the big stuff that really matters to you!**

In the moment, sure, a distraction can be entertaining and put a smile on your face (you sap). But too many distractions make sure you get nowhere in life. **Distractions are like a hole in your gas tank, drip drip dripping all day long, making sure you come to a dead stop on the road of life.** And that's the stuff of suffering, my long-haul trucker of pain! So forget about keeping to your trip plan of life, instead get distracted, pull off the road, coast into that rest stop, and take a nice long nap. Zzzz.

Luckily distractions are plentiful and come in so many forms! Like right now, you're probably thinking about that expired Twinkie in your pantry and wondering if it's still good enough to eat. It's not (in spite of urban myths, Twinkies don't last until the end of time). Even so, you're thinking about that Twinkie, which is distracting you from reading this book. A book that could invariably, inevitably, indubitably change the very direction and destination of your entire life! Is golden sponge cake with creamy filing really worth that? Of course not, and **that's what makes distractions such things of beauty: they cause you to focus on the trivial shit, and ignore the important shit, and thus go nowhere.** And going nowhere means you don't have to exert in any way. Nice! So enjoy that distraction and your individually wrapped loaf of misery!

What are distractions exactly, you ask? Distractions divert your attention away from your intended area of focus. **There are both internal and external distractions. Internal distractions include things like worries, daydreaming, complaining, and that chimichanga bomb fermenting in your gut. External distractions include noise, phone calls, emails, texts, unexpected requests, and a pen light that causes you to jump around trying to catch that glowing dot.**

According to productivity writer Marija Kojic (whose name arguably has more J's than necessary):

- **We experience about 56 disruptions per day**
- **We spend about 2 hours per day refocusing**
- **This leads to 2 or 3 times more errors**

According to Double J, the following are **the most common forms of distractions at work**, which she shamelessly snagged from research from CareerBuilder, and I'm shamelessly snagging from both of them:

- **Mobile phone / texting**
- **Internet**
- **Social media**

- **Gossip**
- **Email**
- **Co-workers dropping by**
- **Meetings**
- **Noisy co-workers**
- **Smoke or snack breaks (damn sheet cake in the breakroom!)**

So, if you're committed to being miserable (your mouth says no, but your actions YES!), don't minimize these distractions and instead let them lead your mind away from anything productive or important. **To remain a miserable and distracted mess:**

- **DON'T turn your phone ringer off during focused work times**
- **DON'T resist the temptation to browse the web every 5 minutes**
- **DON'T limit socializing to lunch breaks**
- **DON'T keep social media browsing to an hour a day**
- **DON'T check email in batches just 2 or 3 times a day**
- **DON'T keep meetings to a minimum number and length**
- **DON'T wear noise-cancelling headphones**

There's another form of distraction that's not simply a shiny object leading our mind elsewhere. There's another more psychologically creepy form of distraction: Safe Problems. And know it or not, you loves you some Safe Problems!

What Is A Safe Problem?

People (i.e. you!) are sometimes not effective because of a "Safe Problem" used as a distraction and excuse for not getting shit done. A Safe Problem can be conveniently blamed, and complained about over and over (you know, like all that whining you do daily?). For instance, if you have a personal goal, you might use a Safe Problem as an excuse to not get into action, like you don't have enough time, or you don't have the right equipment, or so-and-so has to help you and doesn't have the time, or you're too upset to start, or you're duct taped in the closet and can't get out. Excuses, excuses, excuses!

A Safe Problem is a convenient justification, a rationalization, and it's used to take up your mental and emotional energy so you don't have any left for more meaningful goals (also known as Quality Problems). Ex. "I'd love to do (my real goal or Quality Problem) but I don't have time because I'm dealing with (my excuse or Safe Problem)."

What Is A Quality Problem?

A Quality Problem is legit, it's meaningful and worth your time, like a positive opportunity that shows up, or a negative situation that needs to get handled. A Quality Problem is much more important than a Safe Problem. When people come up against a risky decision that causes self-doubt, they will often develop a Safe Problem (how convenient!) that will distract them from making the risky decision (well played!). Thus people hide behind the Safe Problem like a quivering, drooling, distracted fool...and continue to be miserable!

Safe Problems are lingering issues that lie within your control like:

- **Procrastination** ("I'll start tomorrow")
- **Hesitation** ("Hmm, should I get out of the way of this freight train? KABLOOEY!)
- **Logistics** ("I'd write that book, but I can't decide what paper to print it on!")
- **Blaming others** ("My mother! My father! My boss! That guy who keeps looking at me!")
- **Avoiding decisions** ("Thanks for asking me to marry you. Anywho, how's that creme brulee?")
- **Withdrawing** ("Have you seen Bob?")

On the other hand, Quality Problems challenge you to accomplish positive things (and we'll have none of this!). Examples of Quality Problems include:

- **Making a career shift** (Don't do it, you might be happier!)
- **Committing to a relationship** (Forget about it. He/she/they will expect all kinds of things from you!)
- **Starting a family** (Have you actually been around a baby!?)
- **Leaving a negative relationship** (The devil you know is better than, well, change.)
- **Moving** (what if you forget which drawer has the spoons!)
- **Healing physically or emotionally** (If you can walk again, people will expect you to walk again!)

Safe Conflicts

Similar to a Safe Problem, there's also something called a Safe Conflict (and you love conflicts almost as much as Twinkies!). A Safe Conflict is an argument you repeat over and over again, doing battle with an opponent not in the real world but in your crazy-ass mind. It could be a boss, spouse, parent, sibling, friend, a rando in a Prius, whoever. Why would you do this? Because a Safe Conflict is just thinking about the problem, and how the other person is wrong and you are right: it doesn't require any bold action, risky conversation, or effort on your part. It's all in your noggin! Easy peasy. People often think their Safe Conflicts are safe because they don't lead to any risk or loss. But this usually isn't true (thankfully for us miserable souls!). For instance, people often think:

- "I can blame my dad for all my problems, and still be close to him." You really think he doesn't pick up on that vibe?
- "I can hate my boss without it effecting my job." Tell that to the unemployment clerk.
- "I can complain to my girlfriends about my husband without losing him." Honey, he's already gone mentally.
- "My mom and dad always blamed other people for their problems. So it's my parents fault I blame others!" Wow, a Safe Conflict boomerang!

Luckily for those of us committed to being miserable, Safe Conflicts often do lead to big issues and giant losses. If you drift into a Safe Conflict, don't interrupt it, keep that made-up, antagonistic, distracting conversation looping in your head over and over again. Don't talk to the person and work out the issue. Don't take bold action to fix the problem. Just let the conflict fester in your mind. And eventually BA-BOOM your life will explode and a new level of misery will be reached! Nice work, fellow sufferer!

To recap, these are some of the primary ways to focus on trivial shit, be distracted, and thus ineffective:

- There are **internal distractions** like daydreaming that can keep you unfocused and not moving ahead on your goals.
- There are **external distractions** like an unexpected text, phone call, or tap on the shoulder that derails your train of thought.
- There are **Safe Problems** that keep you focused on made-up challenges rather than tackling the real ones that can make a difference in your life.
- There are also **Safe Conflicts** where you duke it out in an imaginary fight in the boxing ring of your mind, rather than taking on any real opponents to your happiness.

The real beauty of all of these distractions is that they hinder us from moving forward and immobilize us in a miserable state! So keep yourself distracted, my miserable unfocused compadre!

A Secret Revealed

To finish this chapter strong, I want to reveal my best kept secret. One that will amaze you in its utter brilliance! This secret, once revealed, will change your life forever. So stay focused, dear reader, and take notes as I divulge this incredible truth!

This secret is... Wait, never mind. There's a cute wittle bunny outside my window! Gotta go!

NOTES

Write Down All Of Your Dreams Here
(So we all can laugh at you!)

_____

_____

_____

_____

_____

_____

_____

_____

_____

_____

_____

_____

_____

_____

_____

_____

Lesson 11:

Never Feel Like You Have Enough

They say enough is enough. Well, I say enough is never enough! **Enough is for the weak, the easily satisfied, the unambitious.** Never be satisfied. Never be grateful for what you have. Never stop grasping desperately for more, like an orange-fingered nerd trying to get his share of the Doritos bag.

Contentment. Satisfaction. Fulfillment. Enjoyment. These are the feelings of those who have forgotten that life should be a fierce battle, a desperate striving, an aching emptiness that needs to be filled, a misery pit that has no bottom, a never-ending pursuit of filling life with MORE!

More, Better, Different

Never-ending insatiable misery is available to you by pursuing More, Better, and Different stuff. Never be okay with what you have, where you're at, or where you're going. Instead seek MORE...more money, more fame, more prestige, more love, more sex, more fatty sugary treats! Also seek BETTER...a better job, better spouse, better kids (yeah, you can admit it). And don't forget to chase down DIFFERENT...don't be satisfied with what ya got, with the same-old-same-old, seek something different, change it up, flip the table of life and let all the dishes smash on the floor. **A life in pursuit of More, Better, Different is a life of exquisite misery...nothing is good enough, not now, not ever. Happiness is always a few inches out of reach. "Just...a little...farther...then I'll be happy."** Ha! Keep reaching, my perpetually unsatisfied friend!

Let's break it down further.

More!

Some people have 10,000 square foot houses. Why don't you have one, dammit? You deserve a McMansion too, right? Who do they think they are? They think they're better than you! Forget the fact that those people haven't seen most of the rooms of those houses in years. It's not about what you need, it's about what you deserve. And you deserve MORE! Ignore the fact that in a house like that you'll need a tracking device on your kids. You still want MORE!

Better!

A few years ago, I had a friend come over to my house for dinner. While there, I caught him seemingly admiring my brand new flatscreen TV. It was 55 inches, and it was my pride and joy — for the moment. I said to my friend "What do you think, cool TV, right?" My friend said smugly. "Yeah, it's nice...for you. Mine is 85 inches." DOAH! I never was satisfied with my TV again. I wanted BETTER! I ignored the fact that an 85-inch TV in my then smallish living room would have seared my retinas and caused a flash fire on my eyelashes. I still wanted WAY BETTER!

Different!

I lived in Cleveland for most of my young life. Then I moved to Phoenix as an adult. Why did I move? Because I lived in Cleveland (bah-dum-tss!). The Midwest was cold, dreary and most importantly, what I had known my whole life. The Southwest was warm, sunny, and brand new! I wanted DIFFERENT! I ignored the fact that in Phoenix, it's so hot, you can bake sticky buns in your mailbox. I still wanted DIFFERENT!

The Hedonic Treadmill

"Psychologists" (don't get me started on them!) say that when us humans experience something positive — a promotion, a new car, remembering we have a year-old bag of Skittles under our bed — there is a rush of happiness. That glee is fleeting (thankfully), and we return to a ho-hum state over time. We then take actions in an attempt to get that happy feeling again. This is the "Hedonic Treadmill." We're all running after self-indulgence and enjoyment.

The Hedonic Treadmill is a metaphor (thank goodness, because we don't like to run) for the human pursuit of one pleasure after another. There's a surge of happiness felt after a positive event, but soon after we return to a baseline state, and so we chase after the next pleasurable experience in order to spike again. But, like a real treadmill, we never get anywhere! How cool is that! As David Byrne said (search him up, Gen Z-ers), "We're on a road to nowhere."

Are you feeling gosh-so-fantastic-thanks-for-asking today? **Don't worry, that feeling may not last long...unless you jump back on the treadmill to chase down the next happy thingy.** To remain miserable, don't do that! Instead, sit on the side of the road to happiness, stay in that place motionless, feel miserable, and maybe some ants will bite you in the ass too.

A word of caution, my committedly miserable pal: **the treadmill applies to painful events too.** When you experience something bad, the negative feelings lessen over time. **An awful event happens, you feel sad or pissed or both for hours or days or even weeks. But eventually, those feelings soften, dissipate, lessen. Dammit!** What's a guy who's committed to misery to do? Keep looking for and finding painful events, even if you have to make them up in your head (brilliant!), so that you continue to suffer continually and consistently. Remember that you're a member of the Misery Mouse Club, and you can find sorrow, even create it out of thin air! Hey there, hi there, ho there, you're as miserable as can be!

Some people think life is like a long, slow jog on a country road, moving along toward a destination. I suggest it is more like intervals on a treadmill: we sprint, we rest, we sprint, we rest. It's not about getting somewhere, it's about those bursts. You can sprint for happiness, over and over again, being fired up in those moments. Or you can sprint for misery, over and over again, suffering in those moments, never feeling like life is what you want it to be. It's up to you. And from the looks of things, you've been turning the misery setting up to 11 on your treadmill. And pulling a hamstring every time!

What exactly is the Hedonic Treadmill?

Our emotions have an equilibrium (sorry for the big word). Joy dissipates. Rage calms. Grief lessens. We return to our base state. That's why many people step back onto the Hedonic Treadmill to run after those good feelings again, or sprint after miserable feelings if that's their familiar emotional state (sound like anyone you know?). Psychologists think this returning to equilibrium is for our survival, like a reset to be ready to deal with whatever shit is coming at us next, whether sabretooth tiger or boss.

Some feelings fade faster than others:

Be aware that all emotions, from joy to rage, can fade quickly or slowly depending on what stimulus triggered them. **Some events cause long-lasting pleasure or pain. Some events cause a quick spike that drops faster than a ham thrown off a building.**

For example, events that cause intense emotional experiences, whether extremely happy or sad, tend to be less long-lasting. Had an intense experience? Enjoy it while it lasts. Soon it will fade faster than a politician's promises, and it will be time to jump back on the treadmill and sprint!

Novelty also wears off fairly quickly. So if you've moved to a new city or taken a new job or traded in your husband for the latest model, you may feel an increase in happiness because you're experiencing something new. But, as you grow accustomed to your new situation, those feelings may subside somewhat. Time to get back on the treadmill like the Jesse Owens of emotional sprints!

Another factor that can influence the duration of your feelings is comparing yourself to others. **Studies show that when you pursue** and get something because other people have it, the happiness you experience wears off swiftly. **However, if you attain something that you value yourself, whether or not anyone else wants it, your satisfaction persists longer.** So, to live in the neighborhood we call misery, forget your own goals, and instead try to keep up with the Joneses next door! Scrimp and save to buy a new car like theirs. Take a lavish vacation like you saw on their Facebook page. Why be happily YOU when you can try desperately to be THEM and thus enjoy only fleeting feelings of happiness?!

Sentimentality can also prolong feelings of happiness. A study found that when people are sentimental about a thing or an event, the happiness stays longer. For instance, when admiring the ashtray your child made for you at camp years ago, the upswell of delight is less about the "beauty" of that misshapen ashtray than it is about the child who made it with her teeny, stinky, awkward hands. So, to optimize your misery, get rid of sentimental items — sweep your house of them – so you don't have those happiness-triggering tchotchkes in your house no more! You can put out your cigarette on your thigh. More misery!

Two flavors of happiness

Watch out for these two sources of pleasure: hedonism and eudaimonia (sorry, more big words). You'll want to avoid them at all costs, Mr. and Ms. Miserable. Put your feet on the sides of the treadmill and let those happiness sources roll by between your legs.

Hedonism

Think of hedonism as enjoyment. Pleasure. It's the immediate good feeling we experience when we do something we like. Food and sex are sources of hedonic pleasure (especially with the right dipping sauces). But any activity can qualify as hedonism, from playing video games to reading this book (which is better than sex, right?!). So avoid pleasurable experiences of all types and you'll be sprinting up a hill of misery!

Eudaimonia

Eudaimonia (don't try to pronounce it, it's impossible) is the fulfillment we experience from pursuing meaningful activities. Examples include finding your purpose in life, helping others, and growing personally. This type of happiness is less susceptible to the treadmill effect. It lasts. Researchers at Western Oregon University (yeah, that's a place) have found that eudaimonic happiness takes longer to fade than hedonic happiness. So if you're sincerely committed to misery (and judging from your flared nostrils you sure the hell are!), you'll want to avoid pursuing your purpose, dodge helping others, and refuse to grow as a person (plus never refill the dipping sauces)!

Happiness (and misery) are in your control

As noted in the film *The Science of Happiness* (watch it on Amazon Prime, and order an ice pack too from Amazon to sooth your eyes from rolling back in your head), **researchers found that you can consciously choose activities and habits to influence 40% or more of your happiness level.** In other words, you have a lot of control over your happiness level and you can increase it by choosing the right activities. To these researchers I say keep your happiness-inducing theories to yourself. Instead, use awful activities and bad habits to turn yourself into a steaming pile of misery! Here's how.

To be miserable, never wrangle your thoughts.

Racing thoughts, free-floating hate, low level rage, an endless mental loop of self-pity – let 'em rip! You don't have time or patience for mindfulness. Meditation is for wusses. Breathing exercises leave you gasping for air. These practices of mindfulness can quiet your mind and align your thoughts. A quiet mind is a happy mind and we'll have none of that! Instead, rage on!

To be miserable, don't grow. Instead, stagnate.

Your sense of well-being is connected to your personal growth and development. According to research from PubMed Central (which is smack dab in the middle of PubMed evidently), **people can have a lasting sense of satisfaction by:**

- Pursuing personal goals
- Envisioning a positive future
- **Immersing in activities that put them in "flow"** (a state of being so completely focused, the rest of the world disappears for a while. This should not be confused with Flo, a character in an insurance commercial.)

So, to be miserable, do that voodoo that you do: the opposite!

- **Don't pursue your goals,** let them be nice ideas you once had, then someone distracted you with funny-face cupcakes in the breakroom.
- **Envision a mediocre or horrible future.** The future isn't a real thing, it's just a story you make up in your head about what's coming next in life. So make up a doozy!

- **Let unimportant things take up all your time.** Get distracted, preoccupied and overwhelmed with the busy-ness of the day. The random phone calls. The spam emails. The gossip at work (she did WHAT with her WHAT?). Never get focused on the things you love or the activities that give your life purpose. Instead, let anyone and anything steal your precious time. Allocate only the remains of your day to your dreams, just the leftover scraps of time, and thus never reach those dreams!

To be miserable, appreciate nothing.

Researchers have found that **appreciation — intentionally being thankful for a positive experience — is linked to an enlarged capacity for happiness. I say anything that's enlarged can't be healthy!** The researchers go on (and on!) to say that appreciation can slow down the Hedonic Treadmill, like pressing the down arrow on the treadmill's screen, so your happiness sprints last longer. As we reflect on and appreciate past events that made us happy, our happiness becomes more consistent and persistent. But if you're truly committed to being miserable, not some slap-happy ignoramus, then you'll steer your mind away from appreciation, develop some impossible-to-satisfy demands of life, and focus on what's missing. **Focus on the holes and you'll become one yourself!**

To be miserable, fly solo.

Studies all over the world, over several decades, point to relationships as a key to long-term happiness. According to this research, the happiest people are those who build supportive relationships, and take advantage of social opportunities in their community. So, **to be ex-**

quisitely miserable, be a lone wolf. Don't reach out to new people, why risk the embarrassment, right? Don't invite the neighbors over for Moscow Mules, they'll think you're a Russian commie weirdo or something. Don't say hi to the guy on the elevator, just stare at the floor numbers. They're fascinating. Don't call that old friend, he should be calling you dammit! Now there's some self-inflicted misery, Lone Ranger!

To be miserable, focus on yourself, not others.

Studies (why are people always studying stuff?!) show that helping others and "being of service" increases long-term happiness. **Self-centered pursuits tend to cause more fluctuations in happiness vs. the lasting pleasure of doing something selfless, which can lead to contentment and inner peace. Zzzzzz. Inner peace is a snoozer! Instead we want an inner war!** Forget "others," focus on yourself, and keep chasing down More, Better and Different, all for your egocentric, greedy self! Gimme gimme!

To be miserable, never treat yourself!

Let's face it, you don't deserve it. That new silky shirt. That cucumber-scented spa day. That ice cream with chunky chunks of chunk. You haven't earned it yet. You'll treat yourself "someday." Sure, **the inability to enjoy simple, hedonic pleasures is a sign of mental health issues.** But let's face it, mental health is overrated. So don't treat yourself to a night out on the town, instead stay home and watch a Telemundo sitcom (even though you don't know Spanish). Don't roll down the windows and crank up the tunes, instead stifle in silence in your car (you don't want the guy in the next car to laugh at you, do you!?). And stick to your raw food diet, even on your birthday: sheet cake is for sissies! You see, occasional indulgences are an ingredient to emotional and mental well-being, and that sounds a lot like happiness, so we'll have none of that thank you! Pass the raw kale, no dressing!

SAVE TIME, DON'T READ THIS QUOTE:

Don't ever save anything for a special occasion. Being alive is the special occasion.

- Power of Positivity

To be miserable, never feel like you have enough.

Let's face it, my miserable friend, you'll never have enough. There's always more, more, MORE! To be miserable, focus on the abyss between what you want and what you got. Keep running on that Hedonic Treadmill. Desperately pursue one quick fix after another in a futile attempt to always be happy. When the feeling fades faster than cheap hair dye, just jump back on that treadmill again and chase down More, Better, and Different. There's a beautiful misery in those awkward futile attempts! Ignore that some kinds of happiness are more durable than others. Ignore the fact that pleasure from selfless acts outlasts selfish indulgences. Overlook that mindfulness, personal growth, gratitude, and relationships can all lead to lasting happiness. No, instead, keep flailing around trying to find happiness in more stuff, better stuff, different stuff! Never realize that "enough" is not somewhere "out there," it's simply a state of mind you can choose. Instead, run, Forrest, run!

NOTES

Write Your Pledge To Lifelong Misery Here
(You should know this one by heart!)

_____

_____

_____

_____

_____

_____

_____

_____

_____

_____

_____

_____

_____

_____

ALWAYS BE YOURSELF. UNLESS YOU CAN BE SOMEONE WAY BETTER.

Lesson 12:

Don't Question Who You Are

P opeye said, "I yam what I yam and that's all that I yam." Truer words have never been spoken by a cartoon sailor. We yare who we yare. **Being a miserable wretch on both land and sea means believing you have an immutable identity, with glaring faults, and you can't change yourself in any way** (even those freakish forearms, sailor man).

Who are you to think you can change or transform into a better self? How dare you think your perception of yourself, your identity, is just made-up anyway, and you can un-make-up your deflating beliefs about who you are? Don't you dare make up more inspiring beliefs about yourself to fuel more success and (gasp!) happiness? No, no, NO! If you have a life-long commitment to being Your Miserable Self (and judging from that high school yearbook pic, you've been miserable for years), you'll want to believe that you are a certain way, and you'll be that certain way for life. Bluto gonna punch. Olive gonna faint. Wimpy gonna wimp-out. Got it? **Some people think they can change, that their identity is mutable, changeable, relative, and so they have the power to question their restricting beliefs about themselves, shift their perceptions about their identity, and begin to believe that they are capable of anything.** To that I say, "That's all I can stands, I can't stands no more!"

To bathe in misery (and that's some warm familiar bathwater for you!), you should believe your identity is permanently fixed, firmly established, not subject to any alteration. **Sure, some people have overcome obstacles to accomplish great things, and thus become something new and, well, better. Rosa Parks. Nelson Mandela. Bruce Wayne. But let's ignore them, shall we?** It's uncomfortable to think our identity is changeable, and we don't like to be uncomfortable. For us miserable folk, it's better to lay on a bed of nails we know than a pillowtop mattress we don't!

Psychologists (a.k.a. highly paid bartenders) believe that one of the strongest drivers in human beings is a continuity of identity. In other words, we all are driven to have our known and familiar identity continue as is. This is true whether we like ourselves or not! This is true even if shifting our identity would serve us well! We want to know ourselves, warts and all. Imagine waking up in the morning, looking in the mirror, and seeing someone else's face! It would be shocking and upsetting (even if a vast improvement).

"Personal continuity" is an important part of identity. **We want to ensure that our self is consistent from one moment to the next.** Yet it has been argued (and we LOVE arguments!) that there is no such thing as a permanent identity. Daniel Shapiro asserts (because, let's face it, what else does he have to do?) that there is no permanent identity and instead there are only "thoughts without a thinker." According to him, this view is based on the Buddhist concept of *anatta*, "a continuously evolving flow of awareness." Malcolm David Eckel states (because he also has time on his hands), **"the self changes at every moment and has no permanent identity" and we are in a "constant process of changing or becoming;" we all have a "fluid ever-changing self."** To that I say, "Shush, all of you, or my Personal Continuity will give you a knuckle sandwich!"

According to the University of Chicago Booth School of Business (and no it's not just a booth, they've got real buildings and everything!), **positive changes are less disruptive to our identity than negative changes.** For example, people think that a woman who changes from being cruel to being kind has revealed her "true self"—that these positive qualities were lurking within her and she has simply revealed who she really is. I say, ignore your positive changes and get back to being your ol' self, Cruella!

Booth's research also shows that **people generally expect improvement over time in themselves, and this does not undermine their continuity of self.** Instead, people generally believe us humans can and should continue to expand, grow and develop throughout life, and these positive changes are incorporated into our identity. We accept ourselves when we expand. To that I say, to keep being miserable, the only expanding you should be doing is around the waistline, and I've got a year-old Twinkie to get you started!

Who the heck are you, anyway?

Wondering who you are? Well, candidly, I've had questions about you since Lesson 1. To help us both out, here's an exercise that can help you get to know your identity, meaning who you think you are, and how you came to those conclusions. Put on your Thinking Cap and get ready for some awkward, uncomfortable, smarmy self-reflection. Let's dig in and discover some miserable no-good self-depreciating stories you've made up about yourself!

Remember when you were a stinky no-good little kid? You were small and vulnerable and needed all kinds of help from others (even to wipe your butt, geesh). You wanted love, approval, and help from important people in your life. Momma. Dadda. Steve from Blue's Clues. **Who or what did you become to get approval and support?**

- Maybe you had to be a helper, always looking out for others.
- Or perhaps you were liked for being a class clown, cracking jokes with accompanying bodily noises.
- Maybe you had to be an entertainer, amusing everyone around you. (I bet you still have those tap shoes!)
- Or an overachiever, constantly exceeding expectations.
- Could you only get approval by being sweet and lovable? (You brown-noser!)
- Were you expected to be a leader? Or a follower?
- Or did you have to be a pretty little princess? (Though hopefully not marrying some old guy just to form an alliance with another kingdom.)

As a kid, was it not okay with others for you to act certain ways? What natural, authentic part of yourself did you push down and deny?

- Could you not be silly and carefree?
- Could you not be unhappy? Sad? Angry? A serial killer? (They expected too much of you!)
- Were you discouraged from being too smart? Or too dumb?
- Were you not allowed to be better than them? (Which was a lot to ask of you, judging from your family photo album.)
- Where you not allowed to be worse than them?
- Were you not allowed to be imperfect? (News flash: you are!)

How cool is it that when you created this life-shaping identity to be accepted, you were just a snot-nosed brat of a kid! You were just trying to fit in, so you jumped to a bunch of crazy half-baked conclusions about yourself. HA! You couldn't have fathomed what repercussions these decisions would have later in life. You didn't realize these decisions, these made-up stories about yourself, were setting a trajectory for your life. Maybe a trajectory similar to Evel Knievel's when he jumped over the Snake River Canyon (spoiler alert, Googlers: he didn't make it!).

Thanks to these toddler-in-the-driver's-seat-driving-400-miles-an-hour identity-shaping moments, there are many common self-imposed identities that keep us in utter misery. Which one is yours? Maybe you even have more than one Miserable Identity (maniacal laugh!). Here are just a few of the most common below. Along with these, I bet you've invented some lulus yourself!

Common Miserable Identities

- I'm a fake! A fraud! A phony! A failure! (Nearly all of us crazy monkeys have this belief!)
- I'm unlovable

- I'm a loser
- I'm lazy
- I'm shy
- I'm obnoxious
- I'm boring
- I'm awkward
- I'm dumb (or is it dum?)
- I'm a know-it-all
- I'm fat
- I'm a weakling
- I'm a tramp (call me)
- I'm a goody two-shoes
- I'm too young
- I'm too old
- I'm (insert your favorite limiting label here)
- I'm a prancing pony (okay, this one is probably particular to me)

Whatever miserable identity you have, you might be wondering what to do about it. **My advice: to stay miserable, do nothing! Leave that misery-inducing self-inflicted wound of an identity undisturbed. Keep slapping those negative or inauthentic labels on yourself!** Don't change your beliefs about yourself for the better. That's going to take effort. What a hassle! That's going to lead to happiness. That's not our miserable goal! Avoid changing to a more uplifting identity. How?

8 ½ Ways To Avoid Shifting Your Identity For The Better

Changing your identity takes work. Um, no thank you! Instead, you do you, and keep doing you, day after day, year after year, until you fall over dead while shopping at Walmart. Cleanup aisle 6. Here's how to stay miserable and avoid lifting a finger to change or expand your identity (the good news: you're probably already doing all of these tips, my miserable palsy-walsy!):

1. **Don't disturb your negative identity:** To remain miserable, let a sleeping dog lie. Don't question your negative identity. Don't spend time reflecting on successes that are contrary to that negative identity. Otherwise, you might start realizing your negative identity isn't really true, at least not all the time, and you might come to new more positive conclusions about yourself. Think you're dumber than a can of Spam? What about those straight A's you got last semester? Think you're antisocial? Who's that friend you're confiding in? You get the idea. Avoid noticing your positive traits that are contrary to your negative beliefs about yourself. On the hotel room door of your mind, hang a giant "Do Not Disturb" sign and let your negative identity sleep!

2. **Avoid thinking about the pleasure of changing, and the pain of not changing:** Imagine a donkey (partly just because it's fun to imagine a donkey). How do you get the donkey to move forward? Two ways. A carrot in front of him, luring him toward that pleasurable first bite. Also a stick behind him, threatening a whack on the behind unless he moves forward. Guess what? You're a donkey (a jackass even!). Reminding yourself of the pleasure of moving forward in life (yum!), and

the pain of standing still (whack!), could actually get you in motion. So, to remain in your current misery, ignore the pleasure of moving toward something better, and the pain of remaining immobile. That whack on the butt will become as familiar as an old friend, you motionless mule you!

3. **Don't pretend improvements to yourself have already occurred:** People often suggest you should "fake it 'til you make it." To them I say, "Fake you!" Even if awkward at first, acting like you are the person you want to be (short of Anna Sorokin crazy shit) can lead to new actions, then new habits, then new success, then a new identity for yourself. Stop that! To remain miserable ol' you, DO NOT pretend the change you want in yourself has already occurred, it just might come true. And that might be thrilling...which is most definitely not misery!

4. **Avoid new experiences that expand who you know yourself to be:** Don't try new things that shake your understanding of what you're capable of. As an example, if you're someone who believes you're shy, don't sign up to give a public speech, or join a group of friends at happy hour, or speak your mind in a conversation. If you do, you might start questioning your belief that you're shy, and even conclude you really aren't shy, and instead you often can be well-spoken, fun, social, and assertive. But being social and assertive might feel something like, well, exciting and fun, not miserable! So you'll want to be sure not to try new experiences of any kind. Don't go chasing waterfalls, stick to the rivers and lakes that you're used to...and drown in misery!

5. **Don't expand your knowledge and skills in areas you want to change:** To stay miserable, don't fill your noggin with new facts, and don't master new skills. New knowledge and new skills can lead to a new identity, a new way of viewing yourself and the world. You'll start to realize you are growing and changing, and your identity will shift accordingly. Instead, slip back down into your comfy cozy couch that's stuffed full of familiarity, ignorance and utter misery. Ahhh, pass the Cheez-Its!

6. **Don't be in a good mood:** People who are in an upbeat, high-energy mood often believe they are rockstars and can do anything. And you know what, dammit, they often do anything. Ugh! Overachievers make the rest of us look bad! The good news is that the opposite is true too. People who are feeling down, sad, or depressed often believe they are nothing, nobody, unable to achieve anything. And having an identity based on the belief that you're nothing is the most miserable of all! Overlook that this isn't true, that this is just BS you made up. Otherwise, you might cheer up, get in action, achieve your dreams, shift your identity, and become...wait for it...HAPPY (PRIMAL SCREAM!).

7. **Don't get others to support your new identity:** Dreaming of getting in shape? To remain your Miserable Self, don't get a workout buddy who holds you accountable to be at the gym. That's just going to lead to action, a new identity, and lots of perspiration. Ick. Dreaming of being a millionaire? Don't get a mentor who's done it already and can coach you every step of the way. That's just going to lead to more money, and money is "bad" according to (insert your favorite judgmental relative

here). If you want to remain miserable (and those pursed lips imply you do!), then don't get others in your work and personal life to support your new desired habits and encourage you to move forward. That's just going to lead to new positive action, and thus a new positive identity. And anything new is scary and threatening! Same old same old, please!

8. **Don't declare a new identity to yourself or others:** Telling others, or even just yourself, about the "new you" could reinforce that new identity, so stop that! If you find yourself believing something new and empowering about yourself, like you really are capable of anything you set your mind to, push those thoughts out of your mind like Playdough through an extruder. Don't say these self-affirming thoughts to yourself or anyone else. Others might agree with you, and their affirmation might lead to BOOM a new positive identity. So shhh! Don't speak to others about your new identity, and don't speak to yourself either, you just might listen.

8 ½. **Don't realize identity is just a made-up story about yourself.** And, whether a positive or negative story, YOU are the author. And what a whopper of a story you've made up about yourself! Whatever you do, don't edit that story, don't pull out an eraser and do a rewrite, you just might write a more powerful main character and a happier ending and we'll have none of that, my miserable autobiographer!

YOUR WORDS CAN CHANGE
THE WORLD! EXCEPT WORDS
LIKE "ANYWHO", WHICH
REALLY DON'T HELP AT ALL.

Lesson 13:

Ignore Your Words

Some people caution us about words. **"Choose your words wisely,"** they say. **"Words matter,"** they go on (and on!). To them I say, "Words, words, words! Blah, blah, blah!" For those of us who know what's what, who are right all the time (and dammit we are!), **words are not something to carefully choose, words are something to cast out like a rockstar throwing sweaty towels to his hyperventilating fans.** Here you go! You're welcome! We love you, Cleveland!

There are two schools of thought about words. This first school believes words should be chosen carefully, consciously, because these words spewing out of our mouth, or rattling around in our mind, shape our reality, our experience of life. The idear is that there's stuff going on in the world...like when a waiter drops a hot macchiato in your lap...and the moment that happens, you describe the situation with words, like "You're a farging icehole!" Once you describe something happening "out there", those words define the experience. That waiter IS an icehole (and probably for more reasons than the spilled drink. Just look at him!). If you would have used different words to describe the Macchiato Incident, you would have had a vastly different experience. For instance, you could have thought, "He probably feels bad about this. I forgive him. Plus, on the bright side, my lap is now warm and tasty!" If you said this to yourself instead, those words would have led to a completely different experience of the same situation. **Your experience of life can be completely transformed by simply changing the words you use to describe it.** But where's the fun in that? Make the guy wrong, ruin his day and yours. Another Venti Misery, barista!

However, there's another more wonderfully sinister school of thought about words. We've all attended this school, we've all been roughed up in its hallways, there's no recess from the misery, and some will never graduate. **This school of thought believes your words are The Truth.** The idear here is that you believe (HA!) that the words you think in your mind, or say with your pie hole, are correct, factual and indisputable, always and forever amen. I've been watching you (you didn't notice me dead-eyed at your kitchen window, did you?), and I've concluded that you believe you are ALWAYS right! Nice work, my delusional and miserable friend! No matter what crazy-ass thoughts you have, or whacked-out words you puke out of your mouth, you believe you are ALWAYS spot on! Therefore your words never need to be questioned, your thoughts never need to be revised, and others' perspectives never need to be considered, because your thoughts, your beliefs, your words are The Truth! Someone has to be right about everything, right?!

Hurtful Words

In a neuroscience experiment, Maria Richter and her team of scientists (think Minions) monitored people's brain responses to negative words that were thought silently or spoken out loud. **The study proved that negative words release hormones in the body that cause stress and anxiety. A misery cocktail!**

Similarly, another study by J. Lodge, D. K. Harte, and G. Tripp found **increased anxiety in children with higher rates of negative self-talk.** Self-bullying! It's like giving yourself a mental black eye!

Happy Words

In their book *Words Can Change Your Brain*, Dr. Andrew Newberg and Mark Robert Waldman (the Sonny and Cher of neuroscience) said that positive thoughts can literally change one's reality. They write, "By holding a positive and optimistic [word] in your mind, you stimulate frontal lobe activity. This area includes specific language centers that connect directly to the motor cortex responsible for moving you into action. And as our research has shown, the longer you concentrate on positive words, the more you begin to affect other areas of the brain." Geesh! Brainiacs talking about brains. Is there anything worse!? They go on and on about how over time, positive thoughts change functions in the parietal lobe (yeah, it's a thing), which begins to shift our perception of ourselves and others. **By using positive words, we change how we perceive ourselves and the world around us.** Yep, our words can shape our reality and can change our life experience for the better. **But for those of us who are committed to being miserable, luckily the opposite is true too: negative words can change our life experience for the worse!**

As you can see, words can describe the outside world and shape our experience and perception of what's going on out there in the wild. However, **words can also describe things closer to home... yep, words can define what you think of little ol' YOU!** The good news: you are doing a bang-up job of using words to beat the living daylights out of yourself! Way to go, my self-inflicting friend! You actually BELIEVE those words you say about yourself! "I'm a stupid-head. I'm a dumb-ass. (Good job! You criticized both ends of you!) I'm ugly. I'm fat. I'm a loser. I can't get my ass in gear." (You talk about your ass a lot!). You beat the tar out of yourself with words every day...and you're the one making up those words! Heehee! Way to write some misery-inducing, soul-crushing pulp fiction about yourself!

There are words you think about yourself privately. For instance, throughout your day, and even at night when you're alone in your bed, you review the moments of your day, and criticize yourself and every action you took. Nicely done! This is one of the most common and effective ways to be absolutely miserable: a non-stop flow of criticism of yourself in your mind, using that little voice in your head to heckle yourself like you're some hack on stage at a bad comedy club. Keep it up! Keep throwing those mental tomatoes at yourself and you'll have a lifetime ticket to this comedy show from hell!

There also are words you say about yourself out loud to others. You know, those moments you verbally punch yourself in the face in front of onlookers, talking smack about yourself to friends, family, your gynecologist, whoever. Talking bad about yourself to others, any others, is an effective technique to maximize the misery in your life. You'll want to work hard to convince not just yourself, but others as well, from close friends to randos, that you're a no-good, drooling, ineffective, two-faced, conniving, blub-bery, back-boobed, hideous, foot-faced, dumb-as-a-box-of-hammers MEGA-LOSER! Once these others are convinced you suck, they can give you hell too. A verbal pile-on!

However, if you're going to beat yourself up with words, you gotta get better at it. You gotta become OUTSTANDING at using words to describe yourself as abysmal. And I'm here to help.

So far, the words you've been using to criticize yourself are a good attempt, but let's see if we can level up the effort. You currently might be using self-deprecating words (maybe even self-defecating words!) like the following.

Common words of self-criticism include:

- **"I'm so stupid!"**
- **"What an idiot I am!"**
- **"What the hell was I thinking?"**
- **"Why am I such a loser?"**
- **"I'm so ugly/fat."**
- **"I'm too short/tall."**
- **"I'm a bad person."**
- **"No one likes me."**
- **"I am such a failure."**
- **"My life sucks."**
- **And the mother of all self-criticism: "I'm not good enough!"**

A solid effort, you! However, you can do even better with some coaching. **Let's take it to the next level by using words even more**

creatively to sucker punch yourself! This is possible because it's all made up anyway. There's nothing really true or factual about any of these statements, so we can make up anything and everything we want, including even more hurtful statements about how you suck, and how you suck at sucking. Some goody two-shoes make up kind and encouraging things about themselves, which motivates them, puts steam in their stride, and keeps them humming along throughout the day. But if you are dedicated to being miserable (judging from those teary eyes you are!), then you can make up words that really bitch-slap you on a regular basis...minute by minute even!

To be even more miserable, use these more imaginative self-criticisms on yourself:

- "I need to check Amazon and see if they have a life for sale."
- "In pics, I'm ugly. In the real world, I'm also ugly."
- "I'm so unimportant, when I talk to myself I say 'Hey you!'"
- "People say someday I'll go far. When I do, they want me to stay there."
- "I'm such a jerk, even I won't talk to myself!"
- "With a face like mine, I should sue my parents."
- "Being myself is a bad decision."
- "My phone charge lasts longer than my relationships."
- "Money talks. Mine says, 'b-bye!'"
- "My life can't fall apart because it was never together."
- "Yeah, I exercise. I run away from my problems."
- "I used to be indecisive. Now I'm not sure."

- "I tried to donate my body to science, but they said no thanks."
- "I make bad decisions even without drugs or alcohol."
- "I hit rock bottom, then start drilling."

Now THAT'S how you insult yourself! Use your words like a champ to give yourself a one-two punch...then three and four! **Overlook the fact that you could also use words to describe the good in yourself, encourage yourself, and comfort yourself.** Ignore that the words you think and speak can be chosen carefully to uplift you instead of tear you down, appreciate you instead of criticize, give you hope instead of despair. Pay no attention to the fact that these words are all made up, and you can make up anything you want about yourself and your circumstances. Discount the idea that it's a matter of focus... that there's both good and bad in anything, including yourself, and **you make a choice moment to moment what you're going to focus on — the good, the bad or the ugly — in yourself and life.**

Like it or not, you are the author of these words. You get to either choose your words consciously or let your word habits take your life on a wild runaway ride of pain. What words are you going to choose? What story about yourself, and life, are you going write? What character are you going to play in this tale? Will your story have a happy or miserable ending? It's all made up. So make up a humdinger!

NOTES

Write Your Thoughts Here
(Which in your case may mean leaving it blank!)

ALWAYS FORGIVE AND
FORGET. WHICH SHOULD
BE EASY BECAUSE YOU
CAN'T EVEN REMEMBER
WHAT YOU HAD FOR
BREAKFAST.

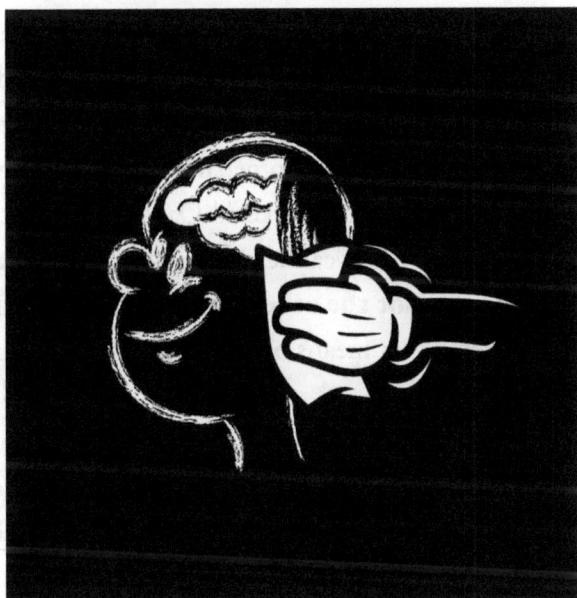

Lesson 14:

Never Forgive. Never Forget.

Forgive my ass! Forgiveness is overrated. People suggest you forgive and forget that awful no-good thing someone did to you. Let it go they say. Move on they say. Let bygones be bygones they say. I say HELLS NO! I ain't forgetting nothing! You wrong me, I'll plot for years to get my revenge, like Al-Qaeda or the cast from *Full House*. Forgiveness is a sign of weakness! **Sure, bottling up anger and resentment hurts me, not the other person.** That's not the point. I need to be right, even if that means being miserable. I'll dig in my heels until they bleed.

My miserable advice: never forgive others. Some people say you should love people for who they are, and who they are not. I say, dislike others for who they are and who they are not – they're really not that great! **Forgiving others means accepting their icky flaws, awkward difference, and lame imperfections. Um, no.** You're better than that (and them!). Instead, step over the fact that perfection has never been achieved by any human. Choose to have lofty ideals, and insist others meet them, no matter how pie-in-the-sky and unobtainable. Insist others get better at, well, everything, so you can finally be satisfied with them. Forgive them for nothing. Insist they quit sucking!

Along with never forgiving others, also never forgive yourself. You also suck. You can and should be doing so much better. Step it up already! Motivate yourself with self-criticism! Beat yourself into submission! Ignore the fact that you've been criticizing yourself for years, and it hasn't changed your performance one smidge. Instead, continue to hold yourself to impossible standards, being a harsh judge, unforgiving jury, and guilt-ridden defendant all in one, conducting a never-ending trial of yourself. Spoiler alert: you're guilty of being an imperfect human being. So to be miserable, continue punishing yourself for this heinous crime! The good news: you're already doing a great job of mentally waterboarding yourself! Keep it up, my miserable jailbird!

Living a miserable life means never completing with painful events of the past. What does it mean to be complete? When someone is truly complete with an event of the past, the past has no constraint on how that person acts in the present. The past is left in the past where it belongs. There are no lingering resentments, regrets or unfinished business. But where's the fun in that?! It's such an energy rush to

> **A disco ball is just hundreds of pieces of broken glass put together to make a magical ball of light. You're not broken, you're a freaking disco ball!**
> - The Real Healing
>
> **Disco is dead.**
> - Me

remain incomplete with the past, enraged by others and their past offenses, letting their past actions fester in our minds like a smoldering ash heap, leading to feelings of hate, bitterness, and let's be honest here, power. Our clenched fists, grinding teeth and furrowed eyebrows make us feel powerful and dominant over our offenders. And that my friend is one reason why you don't complete with the past, and instead drag it into your present over and over. **You'd rather be miserable and right than happy and forgiving.** How beautifully incomplete and wonderfully painful. Keep up the good work, my miserable colleague!

True story. My father once didn't talk to his brother (my uncle) for several years. It was a wonderfully unnecessary grudge over nothing! Well played, Dad! Our family is Italian-American, and I can say from experience that because of our cultural background, my family is especially astute at holding grudges for extended periods of time. Here's what happened in this particular instance. My father went over to his brother's house to visit. While Dad was there, my uncle did something unforgiveable! He didn't offer my father...wait for it...a drink! Not a Pepsi. Not a coffee. Nothing! How dare he! My father felt slighted, disrespected, undervalued and unloved. Rightfully so! Who does my uncle think he is not offering a refreshing beverage to his esteemed guest, right?! That's the stuff of lifelong feuds! That's deserving of the silent treatment for years! No drink? Not hot or cold? Not flat or bubbly? My father barely talked to his brother for the next 3 years. Nice job, daddy-o! Way to overlook the possibility that my uncle simply didn't think to offer a drink. Or maybe my uncle was out of Pepsi products (whether sugared or artificially sweetened) or coffee beans (ground or instant) and was embarrassed about his tragic shortcoming. Or maybe my uncle really (REALLY!) needed to go somewhere else and had to keep the visit short. Who knows? My dad never asked. It's always best to jump to negative conclusions vs. gather the actual facts. So this Cold (Pepsi) War lead to several years of suffering for my father, his brother, and their families. No forgiveness. No understanding. No sympathy. No giving of the benefit of the doubt. Nope. Instead, the absence of just 8 ounces of liquid led to a whopping 3-year grudge. Now that's an efficient production to misery! Salute!

As you can see, **regrets, resentments, and unfinished business weigh on us**. Those who complete with the past can live life more effortlessly in the present. Those who have incomplete business live life in a suffering state, forever haunted by the ghost of Christmas Past. How exquisitely miserable, Ebeneezer!

One form of unfinished business is communications we regret. Meaning, shit we've said we wish we could take back. We often wish we could stuff those words back into our mouth like a champ at a hot dog eating contest. However, We The Miserable believe one can never really take back words. Once they are out there, heard by others, it's too late, so there's no need to apologize to others, no need to forgive ourselves for the misstep. Instead, go into Deny & Defend mode! Either sweep it under the rug and pretend it never happened, or go all-in and defend your misinterpretation 'til death. "I never said that!" "You took it the wrong way!" "Besides I'm not wrong, you deserved every word of it!" HA! Way to add more hurtful words to your previous hurtful words to make yourself and others even more miserable! Word to your mother!

Another form of unfinished business is withheld communications. Meaning, important conversations we haven't had the balls to say out loud yet. A communication undelivered can weigh on our mind, drain our energy, and distract us from other important tasks in our life like shopping for organic low-carb gluten-free vegan muffins (good luck). These withheld communications can be with people we see every day, like our wife who we want to ask about that dwarf duct taped in her closet. These withheld communications can even be with people that aren't alive anymore, like a baker friend who passed away before we could tell him we loved his nut loaf (and not just as a euphemism). Messages we've not delivered to others can be burdens on our minds. We try to hide away these unsaid messages, but they keep haunting us, taunting us, showing up again and again uninvited, like yet another season of *America's Got Talent!*

For those of you who want to complete with the past, here's an exercise for you milquetoasts (but **I don't recommend this unless you're clearing space for new, fresh regrets!**). For those of you who are committed to letting the past fester in your life, don't even glance at this exercise, let alone do it!

How to Complete With The Past:

First, List Your Unfinished Business. Write down all the stuff you're incomplete with. Write fast and furious, and don't edit or candy-coat your thoughts. Write it down raw. This list should include (because you've undoubtedly done all of these evil deeds):

- Regrets for things you've done
- Regrets for things you've not done
- Grudges you have with others
- Grudges others have with you
- Words you wish you could stuff back in your mouth

- Words you need to say but haven't had the cojones
- Shit people said you won't let them take back
- Shit people said they refuse to take back
- Opportunities missed
- Opportunities taken that didn't work out
- *Dancing With The Stars* (we all regret this)

Then, choose a few of the juiciest ones...the stuff that haunts you like a needy, clingy codependent ghost. Next, do whatever you need to do to complete with these past events. Apologize to the person. Do the thing that you've been avoiding. Say what you need to say. Write a letter to that person who passed away. Quit being a coward. Quit being Right. Be done with the past once and for all. Leave your present squeaky clean (and ready to be polluted with new resentments and regrets, my miserable trash collector!)

If this exercise includes communicating That Thing You Can't Say to Someone — it may be apologizing, it may be admitting you were hurt (wuss) — be unattached to the other person's response. It's not about how they react. You're doing this to free your mind and soul. What they decide your words mean to them is their business, not yours.

Sometimes this exercise includes forgiving ourselves (I'm suppressing my gag reflex over here). Give yourself a pass. You're not perfect. No one is. Remember Tom Cruise jumping on Oprah's couch? Yeah, no one is perfect, not even Mister Perfect. You're human (though we wonder about Tom Cruise).

Sometimes this exercise above includes taking action. Like delivering the communication you've been avoiding. Or apologizing for your hurtful words. Or moving forward where you've been frozen in the past, like finally starting that cosplay costume knitting club (lovely). However, sometimes this isn't possible. **If there truly is no opportunity for a do-over, there's still something you can do to complete with events like this. Declare yourself complete.** Simply say out loud or in your mind, "It's in the past. There's no way to undo it. I declare myself complete. I'm moving on now, into my future." Completion is a phenomenon that lives in language. Speaking in part creates our reality. So, to be complete with something, declare yourself complete. Use your words. After you have acknowledged your mistakes, examined your disappointments, forgiven others for their shortcomings, and forgiven yourself for that whopper of a sin (you did WHAAT in a public restroom?!), declare yourself complete. Let the past go. Leave it behind like a grease-soaked doggie bag from an awful restaurant your friend dragged you to.

Once you've finished the exercise above, and you're truly, authentically complete — you've forgiven yourself, accepted others, shaken off life's disappointments, and put the past behind you – **there's still good news for those who are committed to being miserable! You've created space for some new regrets and resentments!** So get busy! Start anew! Pile on some new unfinished business! Stack the disappointments! Begrudge others! Bemoan your every decision! Resent and regret with fresh enthusiasm! Judging from those creases in your forehead, you are excellent at this! **So even though you completed some things from the past by doing this exercise, don't learn from it, don't do this exercise over and over again, don't make this a habit, don't make this a new way of life.** Instead, just forget about this forgiveness process, shake it off, find new things to resent and regret, then leave them undisturbed for years. Forgive yourself from ever forgiving again. Forget about forgetting. Misery will be yours for the rest of your life!

YOU CAN'T ALWAYS GET WHAT YOU WANT. BUT IF YOU TRY SOMETIMES, YOU JUST MIGHT FIND A RECENTLY EXPIRED PUDDING IN THE BACK OF THE FRIDGE.

Deny Your Desires
(You Don't Deserve Them)

Quit being such a needy lump of goo! You don't need your needs! Quit wanting your wants! Stop desiring your desires!

Some people say that pursuing our deepest needs, wants and desires will lead to a fulfilling life. "They" say you honor yourself by acknowledging those aches deep down inside (no, not yesterday's double-cheeseburger). "They" tell you to ask yourself uncomfortable questions about what you really want out of life. What are your authentic needs? What are your secret wants? What are your deepest desires? Do you need to quit that soul-sucking job and start a shave ice stand in Hawaii? Do you need to get out of that toxic relationship and be on your own, free as a bird? Do you need to kiss that cute boy/girl/ non-binary? Whatever you need, really need, there's a beauty in honoring it, some people say.

I say different. (Of course, right? You know me by now.) I say pursuing your personal needs is like celebrating the whin-

ey, needy, crybaby inside you. The one that's always whimpering, drooling, pawing for more in life. Be a man (yeah, you ladies too!). You don't need your needs. You've gotten this far without fulfilling them, so why start now? Deny those needs. Push those desires down into your gut like a 12-year-old boy gulping down air to create an epic belch!

SO DUMB & DUMBER:

You can fail at what you don't want, so you might as well take a chance at doing what you love.

- Jim Carrey

George Santayana (no relation to Santa, I checked) said, "Knowledge of what is possible is the beginning of happiness." Nay nay I say. Knowledge of what is possible is the beginning of suffering! Wanting more, needing more, is at the heart of dissatisfaction! BULLSEYE! I would argue (and you know I love to argue) that all misery comes from noticing the difference between what ya want and what ya got. **To be miserable, simply discover what's possible, what's missing, then (hee hee!) do nothing about it! Make no effort to move toward the thing you want.** Just roll around in the giant abyss between your reality and your goals. Don't lift a finger, just notice the difference between the incredible things that are possible and your no-good stinking life. Misery is yours! It's like a gift from Santa(yana)!

Maya Angelou said, "We need joy as we need air. We need love as we need water. We need each other as we need the earth we share." Joy. Love. Each other. Is that all we need, Maya? What about a house way bigger than my friend's? Or lips poutier than my sorority sister's? Or a lifestyle more righteous than my neighbor's? I need those things too! Sure, meeting my needs for joy, love and connection will make me feel happy. However, meeting my need to be better than others will make me feel, well, better than others! **And I (probably like you, reader!) would rather be better than happy!** Maya, you go ahead and serve up that beautiful banquet of joy, love and others. I'll keep flipping that banquet table. I'd rather wait for superiority to be served on a platter. So what that I'll be waiting a long time and might never get to eat.

Billy Graham had to get in on this conversation too, the chatterbox. He said, "Man has two great spiritual needs. One is for forgiveness. The other is for goodness." Oh man, he's so preachy! Look, Billy, I need way more than forgiveness and goodness. Besides, if I go around forgiving people for the crap they did to me, sure, it will unburden me, lighten my load, allow me to be complete with painful past events and move on in peace. I get it. But...if someone did me wrong, I want to get them back! If I forgive them, I'll lose all my motivation to make their life a living hell (it takes a lot of effort to ignore the rest of my life, my goals and my responsibilities, and instead focus on making someone else pay). Yes, I'll be miserable as I plot my revenge, but I'll be RIGHT! And **BEING RIGHT is my ULTIMATE NEED.** I'm willing to burn to a crisp in the eternal fires of Hell if first I can prove to others that I'm SO DAMN RIGHT! Can I get an amen, Billy?!

Human beings (you're likely one or close, dear reader) share common wants and desires. We're more alike than different (even though you've got your own weird-ass spin on things over there). Humans have multiple wants and desires (unlike squirrels, who seem to focus on nuts), and we run around trying desperately to fulfill these wants and satisfy these desires.

For Survival, We Want Things Like:

- Air
- Water
- Food
- Shelter
- Sleep
- Health

For Success, We Want Things Like:

- Wealth
- Prestige
- Attractiveness
- Power
- Friends
- Romance

For Spirit, We Want Things Like:

- Learning
- Wisdom
- Perspective
- Community
- Selflessness
- Pizza (tell me with a straight face you don't want pizza right now)

Sometimes our attempts at acquiring the things needed for Survival, Success and Spirit are ineffective, and so there's...wait for it...suffering! Oh the pain! Oh the agony! So if you're committed to misery (and clearly you are, my long-faced friend!), then you'll continue to **do nothing, NOTHING to meet your desires in these areas.**

Scared about your money situation? To stay miserable, do nothing to make your finances better!

Bored out of your skull? To stay miserable, just rewatch The Office for the 12th time. (Oh, that Dwight!)

Lonely? To stay miserable, keep being overly picky about who can be your friend.

Feeling stagnant? To stay miserable, don't learn something new or try a new experience.

LIAR, LIAR:

"So many of us choose our path out of fear disguised as practicality, what we really want seems impossibly out of reach and ridiculous to expect. So we never dare to ask the universe for it. I'm saying I'm the proof you can ask the universe for it."

- Jim Carrey

Feel like your life doesn't matter? To stay miserable, don't find a way to make a difference in the world.

It's that simple. You have desires. When you don't bother to take action toward your desires, you feel like something is missing. You can deny your desires and pretend they aren't there. That leads to suffering. You can give a half-hearted attempt to meet your desires then sink back into the couch. That leads to suffering. You can blame others for you not meeting your desires. That leads to suffering. You can become impatient with meeting your desires. That leads to suffering. So, your wants and desires can be a fountainhead of misery! They also can be a gushing source of fulfillment – if you take action and make progress towards the things you yearn for. Here's the thing: tak-

ing consistent actions towards meeting your needs, wants and desires gives you hope, lights you up, has you jump out of bed in the morning for another shot at reaching your end goal. You don't have to reach your goal to be happy, you just need to take action and make progress and you'll be excited about life. **So, to stay miserable (like you evidently, wholeheartedly, undeniably want to!), don't take action toward the things you want most!** If you're committed to misery (that grumbling in your tummy says you are!), notice what's missing in your life, and do nothing, take no action, make no progress, just sit there motionless like one of those creepy bronze statues on a park bench frozen in time. And don't bother shooing away the pooping pigeons, they'll add to your statuesque misery!

Lesson 16:

Envision A Horrible Future

Let's start with a shocker. Can you handle it, sparky? **Consider that there is no such thing as the future.**

"But but but...of course there's a future," you say. "For instance, I gotta make that presentation at work next week and I'm dreading that disapproving blank stare from my boss. Then there's that blind date next weekend who I'm sure is "fun at parties." Then I gotta spend the holidays with my family...and hear their radicalized crazy-ass political views! So, of course there's a future, though it's a sucky one!" Whatev. There's no such thing as the future I say.

Many people say the future is in front of them, like they're traveling down a country road and the future is just up ahead. I'd argue that analogy is as shaky as Kim Kardashian on a washing machine. I'd argue that there is no such thing as the future.

If there is such a thing as the future, where is it? I say it's not real. Not tangible. If it is, point to it, grab it, show it to me. You

can't. That's because the future is located in only one place: your mind. The future is just your thoughts. The future is just a made-up story you tell yourself about what's going to happen next in life. You are the author of this story. And you're a terrible writer.

Here's why. **If the future is just made-up stuff, then you can make up anything you want**...a wild fantasy about what wonderful things the future will bring! But you don't. Instead, you make up a future-story that is pathetically small, boring, dim, and unimaginative. You can make up ANYTHING and you make up THAT?!

The "future" is just made-up baloney, and you could be making up better baloney. With fancy mustard on top. But you don't! HA!

The problem with your story about the future is that it's really about the past. Things happened in your past, unpleasant things, painful things, awkward things, dark things, failure-infused things. So you erroneously concluded that what happened in the past was all that was possible in your future too. **That big steaming pile of past wasn't left behind where it belonged. You allowed it to stink up your future too.**

We all are guilty of this delightfully painful sin. We take our experiences from behind us and let them taint what's in front of us. We limit ourselves, relating to the past as if it's going to happen again and again, as if it's all that can happen now and in the future. This leads to a story about the future cluttered with the defeats of the past, tragically limiting what's possible for us moving forward. **If our past is a trainwreck, we assume our future is going to be a trainwreck too. Choo choo BOOM!**

Let's say you're 12 years old and playing in Little League. Your first season, you play terribly. No runs. No hits. Dropped fly balls. You can't even chew bubblegum well. You might not conclude that you need more practice or a better coach, you might instead conclude that you're a terrible athlete, then drag along that belief with you for days, months, even years. That disempowering belief from past events will continue to limit you in the present and future. Because of this erroneous belief, you might not have a fighting chance of being good at sports, or even enjoying sports, for the rest of your life. Way to create misery for a lifetime, my Bad News Bear!

For those of you not fully committed to a Life of Loathing (you creampuffs!), you can stop letting your painful past define what's possible in your present and future. **If you stop envisioning a future that looks just like your past, then your story about your future can be anything you want to make up, full of endless possibilities — whatever you want to have, and whoever you want to be.**

(INSERT VINYL RECORD SCRATCH SOUND EFFECT HERE!) Yeah, no. Don't do that! **If you're committed to being miserable (you are, judging from that Netflix message that keeps popping up asking if you're still watching), continue to repeat your past in the present and future.** Be like Tom Cruise in the film *Edge of Tomorrow*, repeating the same crappy day over and over again, lost in a black hole of time!

A THOUGHT TO AVOID:

When people talk about time-traveling to the past, they worry about radically changing the present by doing something small. But barely anyone in the present realizes they can radically change the future by doing something small.

For those who are determined to pull their head out of this black hole (or any hole), there are steps you can take to consciously create a compelling, exciting, motivating, life-affirming future (which makes my stomach twist even thinking about it). For those namby-pamby readers who want a happy future full of possibilities and rainbows and unicorns farting glitter, here are some steps you can take (hope you trip).

How to Create An Exciting Future (If You Insist):

1. **Decide to put the past behind you.** Meaning, be aware of what happened to you in the past and notice how it's affecting you today. Decide on a new reaction, and even a new meaning or interpretation of those past events.

2. **Take responsibility for yourself.** Only you can take the actions that can move you forward. Ask yourself: what are you holding onto and why? Do you fantasize about what could have been, rather than accept what actually happened? Are you hanging on to the way life once was, rather than focusing on today? Are you holding on to the past as an excuse to remain in limbo? Is lingering in the past helping you avoid taking risky actions on the future you want to make real?

3. **Accept the past as it really was, no embellishments good or bad.** Look at what was so. Mourn your losses. Celebrate your accomplishments. Know that neither mean anything about today – it's a fresh start, and the game of life continues, so get after it! Accept that the way things were is not sustainable. Today is new, different, and it starts now.

4. **Forgive yourself and others.** Forgiveness simply means accepting, not necessarily approving. Instead of spending time and energy trying to make sense of the past, or trying to rewrite it, or understand why it happened the way it did, simply accept past events and move on to another phase of life. Accept yourself too. You did the best you could, even if that wasn't enough. Don't beat yourself up. Just shift your focus towards the future.

5. **Learn lessons from the past.** The past can be a resource, a teacher. Let it inform your decisions, so you can make better choices about your present and future actions.

6. **Ask yourself: who are you now?** Who do you want to be moving forward? What qualities in yourself are you committed to? What talents do you have or want to develop? What do you value? Consciously define who you want to be NOW. Surround yourself with activities and people who support this. Leave the other activities and people behind.

7. **Make a plan for your future.** Determine what's most important to you now and moving forward. What do you want a year from now? Five years from now? What steps can you take to get there? Today? This month? After that?

> **If you don't know where you are going, Alice, any road can take you there.**
>
> - Lewis Carroll (paraphrased)

8. **Once you have a plan, take action.** Any action. The first action. A small action. Do it now. Even small steps will move

you out of the past and into your future. Try something new. Push your boundaries. Step out of your comfort zone. Have beginner's luck. Or fail triumphantly. Either way, you're now in action and living in the present. Define success not as getting your ultimate result, instead define success as taking any action toward your goals.

Remember that the minute you take your first step into the life of your dreams, the first to greet you there will be fear. Nod. Keep walking.

- Brianna Wiest

Wait! Walking toward your dreams might take you right over a cliff! Run back home and hide under the sheets!

- Me

Sure, you can take steps toward an exciting future, but where's the misery in that?! Instead, to remain in misery (it's a comfortable and familiar place, no?), keep yourself locked up in that mental jail you're in, the bars made of your many past defeats, prior pain, and erroneous conclusion that nothing more is possible in the future. Lay down on your jail cell's cold cement floor, knowing you can't go anywhere, right? Keep life the exact way it's always been, full of disappointments, inaction, and frustration. Keep yourself jailed in the past and make it a life sentence. The ironic thing is, the key to the door is right in your hand, like it's always been. Instead of using it on the lock, use the key to scratch some obscenities on the prison wall. That will make a big difference!

IF YOU LOOK FOR TROUBLE,
YOU'LL FIND IT. MAYBE
SOME MISSING EARRINGS,
TOO.

Lesson 17:

Look The Other Way

'll admit it, I saved the best for last. If you are truly committed to being an Elite Miserable, then this chapter is you. It's next level stuff!

If you follow the advice of this chapter, you can up your miserable game, take it beyond your lonely singular self, and help make the ENTIRE WORLD miserable! Yes, little ol' YOU can help make everyone, everywhere, miserable! And, get this, not just now, but for years, even centuries to come! Imagine being among those who laid the foundation for a miserable world, where everyone suffers on a regular day-to-day basis forever more. You would be a hero among Les Misérables, a historical (and hysterical) figure who set in motion the most miserable period in human history! I'm so proud of you! Don't make me tear up.

What, pray tell, can you do to accomplish this herculean task and earn this honor? It's simple, yet so powerful. Just do this. Look the other way.

Consistently. Perpetually. Unstoppably. Unflappably. Look the other way. When there is an issue that alarms you, ignore it. When there is a cause you care about, don't bother with it. When there is trouble, overlook it. When there is a challenge, fogettaboutit. When there is hurt, rub salt in it. And a dash of Sriracha sauce too.

This "look the other way" gameplan starts with you. When you have a problem, when you suffer, when you feel miserable, look the other way. Deny it. Ignore it. Pretend the problem isn't there. Do nothing to improve your situation. Misery will be yours. Credit cards maxed out? Get another one! Lonely? Who needs 'em! Hurt? What pain! Victimized? He didn't mean it! Dissatisfied? You don't deserve more!

Your goal is to earn the new nickname Cleopatra. Because you're now the Queen of Denial.

Once you've denied your own problems and looked the other way, you can move on to other folks. Got a loved one who's suffering? Look the other way! Offer no help. In fact, criticize them a bit for not handling their shit better. Layer suffering on top of suffering. Brilliant! No need to stop with people you know intimately. What about randos? Like that old lady who's struggling to open a heavy door? Roll your eyes visibly at her! Come on, Meemaw, put your back into it! Ignoring others' suffering is a double whammy: the other person continues to suffer, and you get to suffer because you know damn well you should help but don't! It's like a Buy One Get One Free offer at the Misery Store! Don't slip in the puddle of tears on the store's linoleum floor.

I know, I know, the cliched old lady who can't open the door is as two-dimensional as Nicolas Cage's acting. Real life is more complex than this. I get it. Since you're now a Method Actor of Misery, let's go deeper. **Let's say you have a friend, and she's in a toxic relation-**

ship. **You could let her know you're there for her, remind her she deserves the best in life, share your perspective, shine light on her blind spots, to help her avoid more suffering, and move on to a more healthy, happy life. But instead you do nothing!** You look the other way. You ignore her ticking timebomb of a relationship, letting your friend flounder in ineffectiveness. You don't want the responsibility of mucking with her life. "I don't want to meddle." What a crock! You don't help because you're afraid that if you try you might make your friend mad at you, so you do nothing. NOTHING! And you describe her as your bestie! HA!

Sure, you can look the other way with your own problems, and your friend's problems, but there's a bigger fish to fry (and we love anything fried!). **You can look the other way with societal problems, global problems, everyone problems!** Us humans have this urge to take on these larger issues and help solve them for everyone's benefit. We all want to be part of something bigger. So, to not get involved with your pet peeve, your passion, your cause, is looking the other way from what's important to both YOU as well as OTHERS. A twofer. Brilliantly played!

There are so many causes you could care about. Children's charities. Reproductive rights. Animal cruelty. Immigration issues. Substance abuse. Mental health. Spirituality. Hunger. Fair elections. Gun safety. Alzheimer's. LGBTQ+. Education. Curing cancer. Stopping underground cat juggling. The list goes on and on. The point is... don't get involved with nothing! Look the other way so hard, you hear that popping sound in your neck.

If the park up the street is overrun with graffiti, and you wish it were different, to remain miserable, don't gather some neighbors and some paint and make the park look new again. Live with that 8-foot pee-pee painted on the playground wall, right? Who has time for cleaning up a playground!? You've got to binge-watch all the episodes of *Is It Cake?*.

If political news makes you want to flip a table (plus its chairs!), and you don't get involved, and look the other way (toward that variety pack of Fritos presumably), what a miserable apathy you've got there! What a monumental, life-defining, of-the-utmost-importance problem to ignore! I feel your reaction. "Politics, ugh, don't even go there!" YES, that's exactly the right reaction! That "don't go there" reaction is a form of looking the other way! Great job! **Ignore the gigantic elephant in the room that's trampling all over your country. Ignore the mangy jackass that's taking a dump on us citizens.** Look the other way. Forget about it. It's not YOUR job to wrangle the elephant and donkey, right? Ignore the fact that you and the country are the last things on the self-absorbed minds of these beasties. What can you do, right? There's a "them" out there that will take care of this, won't they? Why have intelligent conversations about issues, and possible solutions, when you can simply cheer for your favorite animal, and hate the other one? Why brainstorm on how best to solve our country's problems?

FUN FACT ABOUT "THE ELEPHANT IN THE ROOM":

It's an idiom about a controversial issue that's obvious but no one wants to discuss because it's uncomfortable. In 1814, poet Ivan Krylov wrote a story "The Inquisitive Man" where a man goes to a museum and notices tiny details in the artwork but fails to notice an elephant in the museum.

Why open your mind to other perspectives? Why watch the debates? Why attend a town hall? Why bother voting? Why volunteer for your candidate? Why peacefully protest? Why educate your friends and family? Why work toward positive change? Why take your focus off of this futile cock fight, and instead focus on the issues and solutions? Look the other way, right? Who cares that your country is starting to stink like a unkept zoo!

Believe it or not, there's another issue, one that, if ignored, can potentially cause misery on an even larger scale, and for years to come! No, I'm not talking about the on-again off-again offering of the McRib sandwich (make up your mind, Hamburger Clown!). No, **I'm talking about climate change. If issues with the environment have your anxiety level going through the ozone, yet you don't lift a finger to help, then I am green...with envy!** Way to look the other way and help make you and others miserable! Like you, so many people are looking the other way while our environment goes to hell in a handbasket! Our planet might be becoming uninhabitable, meaning us humans could go the way of the pterodactyl, so we might want to do something about this, no? Some people are aware of the issue, care deeply about it, yet...wait for it...DO NOTHING! Other people look the other way and deny the problem even exists, and actively fight those who try to address environmental problems. Way to go, you masters of misery! This is the zenith of suffering, to not only ignore something that would kill us all (yes our species and others, even elephants and donkeys), but to also fight those who would work to solve the problem and reverse the pollutants that are turning our world into a Jiffy Pop Popcorn pan. Way to look the other way so hard you get whiplash! Now get some marshmallows and roast them as the world burns!

Maybe you really do care about the environment, but you're just not willing to take a hard look at animal agriculture. Brilliantly misery-inducing! Here's why. According to the University of Colorado Boulder (they're at such a high altitude they might be suffering from oxygen deprivation), "Animal agriculture produces 65% of the world's nitrous oxide emissions which has a global warming impact 296 times greater than carbon dioxide. Raising livestock... generates nearly 15% of total global greenhouse gas emissions, which is greater than all the transportation emissions combined." Sure, this statistic disturbs you, and you care about the issue, but you still do nothing about it, you still want a double cheeseburger, am I right?! Have a side of misery with that!

Instead, maybe you're

(Quick, Look The Other Way!)
Things You Can Do to Save the Planet:

- **Plant trees: removes carbon and shades your house.**
- **Install solar panels on your roof.**
- **Sign up for renewables from your utility.**
- **Buy an electric vehicle.**
- **Walk your kids to school, not drive.**
- **Live close to where you work.**
- **Go to many destinations in one trip.**
- **Use low-VOC paints.**
- **Dispose properly of hazardous waste.**
- **Don't flush unused medications.**
- **In summer, close shades to block sun.**
- **In winter, open curtains to let sun in.**
- **Buy washable clothes to avoid dry cleaning.**
- **Use biodegradable baggies and straws.**
- **Use LED lightbulbs.**
- **Turn off lights not being used.**
- **Buy local & reduce transportation emissions.**
- **Use natural cleaning formulas.**
- **Buy recycled products.**
- **Vote for green candidates.**

freaked out about Artificial Intelligence or A.I. You're afraid that the droids are going to take over the world (let's face it, we've all been suspect of technology ever since we realized a calculator could spell "hello" upside down). When A.I. first burst onto the scene, more than 1,000 technology leaders immediately signed an open letter warning that A.I. presents "profound risks to society and humanity." Within 3 months, the list of signatures grew to over 30,000. No one asked for my autograph though, the nerve!

Where did all these mad panics and night sweats about A.I. come from? **Artificial Intelligence can generate inaccurate, false, biased and even toxic information. A new age of misery has been born!** OpenAI's ChatGPT, Google's Bard, and other systems made headlines for their ability to answer questions, write prose, generate code, create images, and even carry on conversations. (Hmmm...no making of waffles yet.). But these systems can get facts wrong and make up information called "hallucinations." (See, you're not the only one that makes up shit!) Experts are concerned that people will rely on A.I. to make important decisions, seek medical advice, get emotional support, and riskiest of all, decide where to get the best jalapeno poppers! Thus A.I. can spread disinformation like never before. Burn, baby, burn! **Plus many people are fearful A.I. will lead to job loss. Researchers estimate that 80% of the U.S. could have their work tasks impacted by A.I.** If you find yourself scared shitless about A.I., and don't take steps to adapt, what a miserable reaction that is! Simply look the other way. Ignore that the world is changing. Don't help steer things in the right direction. Workers, do you think your current skill set will be enough to keep you in a good job in the future? Tell that to the droids you'll be serving coffee. Executives, do you think you can ignore the human impact of your decisions, and simply go for the money grab? Great job creating an Orwellian future. To bring on a digitally-induced, utterly-miserable future, look the other way from A.I. until society comes apart at the seams!

Dear reader, my last and perhaps most important coaching to you is this. Look the other way from this book! If you've read between the lines and somehow learned something from this book (despite my warnings!), and these new insights have the potential to help you be more fulfilled or happy in life, look the other way and forget about this book and all that you learned, for badness' sake!

If you've read my coaching about how to be miserable, and decided you wanted the opposite, that you wanted to be...ugh...happy (wimp!), let those new thoughts slip away like Jack slipping into the icy ocean water in the film *Titanic*.

Similarly, if you've learned from other self-help or motivational books, seminars, audio programs, and classes past or present, my advice is: stop thinking so hard and crack open another bag of Funyuns!

Forget all the lessons, all the wisdom, all the distinctions that could transform your life for the better. Cuz you and I are not about reaching a better life, my miserable friend, we're about keeping things the same way they've always been, even if awful. Not sure that's true? Look at your track record! You haven't bothered much to stop your momentum toward misery so far in life, why start now?

We've gone over a shitload of stuff in this book (I've measured it with scientific instruments. It's a shitload, maybe even a shitload and a half). **Here's a summary of the miserable lessons from this book you'll want to remember (and do the opposite if you're a goody-two-shoes!):**

1. Start Many Things. Finish Nothing. (Instead of getting in action, continue moving, and being unstoppable)
2. Be In A Bad Mood Often (instead of actively putting yourself in a good mood by consciously choosing mental thoughts and physical activity that create better emotions)
3. Interpret Things In The Worst Way Possible (instead of noticing that your negative stories are just made up, and you can make up better stories)
4. Believe Life Has Meaning With A Capital M (instead of noticing that meaning isn't absolute because it's not "out there," it's you that creates the meaning)
5. Appreciate Nothing (instead of being grateful for everything)
6. Learn To Be Helpless (instead of realizing you are as powerful as you decide to be, and can accomplish anything you set your mind and heart to)
7. Remember: You're Da Man, So Go It Alone (instead of tapping others who have knowledge, perspective, or skills that you don't)
8. Ask Bad Questions (instead of asking powerful questions that lead to better answers and results)
9. Take, Don't Give (instead of helping others, and thus feeling the joy of making a difference)
10. Focus On Trivial Shit (instead of noticing how this distracts you from what's really important in your life)
11. Never Feel Like You Have Enough (instead of appreciating the abundance all around you)
12. Don't Question Who You Are (instead of discarding negative beliefs about yourself, and creating a new and more powerful identity)

13. Ignore Your Words (instead of choosing your words carefully, and thus shifting your perception of reality for the better)
14. Never Forgive. Never Forget. (Instead of leaving past challenges in the past, and moving into the future unburdened)
15. Deny Your Desires (instead of honoring your wants and desires and working to fulfill them)
16. Envision A Horrible Future (instead of realizing the future is just a story you make up, so you might as well make up a good one)
17. Look The Other Way (instead of being brave enough to look reality right in the eyes and work toward positive change)

Thank you for going on this journey towards misery with me! Even before you started reading this book, you were already accomplished in your ability to make yourself and others truly and utterly miserable. That said, there's always more misery available to you! Get in there and dig, you can do it! Find new ways to interpret everything around you as awful and no good. Ignore the fact that you have the ability to make your life better, and also the ability to love and appreciate whatever shows up, good or bad. It's all up to you. What kind of life do you want to experience, my miserable friend?

You see, this book was a devious trick. GOT YA! You now have something that, if not used, can lead to incredible levels of misery. You now have new knowledge! New awareness! New understanding! **You, my insufferable mess of a friend, are out of excuses! HEEHEE! Knowledge, without action, is perhaps the most miserable thing of all.** Leaving the concepts of this book behind, like they were nothing more than some interesting ideas, some intellectual exercises, and not using them, not taking action in your life, is the most miserable result of all from reading this book!

You've finally been bitch-slapped awake. Are you just going to crawl back into bed and fall back asleep? Night night!

To have this book — and all the new insights, all the epiphanies, all the ah-ha moments, all the emotions stirred up — lead to nothing more than you saying, "Huh, that was interesting. Anywho..." then return to your bag of pork rinds is an epic fail, leading to the most Miserable You imaginable! You're welcome.

In other words, I just gave you a shiny new sledgehammer to bonk yourself on the head with for the rest of your life! Are you gonna take it? I bedazzled it and everything!

• •

TELL ME:
How do YOU make yourself miserable?
Share your funny and inspiring stories at
Miserableyou.com
or Facebook.com/miserableyoubook

• •

ABOUT THE AUTHOR

So, who's this **Ron Mileti guy, right?** Why should you care about what he wrote here? Well, he's not just some guy on the street. Ron is an **award-winning writer** and an **International Life Coach & Business Trainer** with a prestigious organization, helping people around the world get what they want from life. Ron has led **thousands of coaching sessions with people all over the world**, from Switzerland to the U.S. to Bermuda to Columbia, from 18 to 80 years old, **from truck drivers to CEOs to TV celebrities.** Ron's mission is to help people do what they thought was impossible.

How did Ron get here? He has been involved in self-help and transformational programs for most of his life. He read his first self-help book ***Think And Grow Rich*** **by Napoleon Hill** when Ron was just 12 years old (if you knew his family, you'd understand why). Later, Ron read more books and listened to audio programs from authors like **Wayne Dyer, Norman Vincent Peale**, and others, and participated in live events and seminars from **Landmark Worldwide** and more. To go pro, Ron first graduated from the **Robbins-Madanes Training, the official coach training school of Tony Robbins and Cloe**

Madanes. Then Ron also completed **hundreds of additional hours of training with master coaches and business trainers** with a notable organization. Ron also earned a Bachelor of Arts from **University of Notre Dame**, and an **MBA** from John Carroll University.

All this education and training lead to Ron's work as a consultant to **Bob Proctor**, speaker, author, and most famously involved in the **book and movie *The Secret*.** This also lead to Ron's work with **Kyle Cease, a comedian** featured on **Comedy Central** who left entertainment to become a motivational speaker.

But this isn't what Ron did for most of his career. He was the founder and president of a digital marketing agency, working with clients and brands like **the Academy of Television Arts & Sciences (the Emmy Awards people), Emergen-C Vitamin Drink Mix, American Greetings, Disney, Cartoon Network, NFL, Hallmark Channel, Lifetime,** and many more. A few years ago, Ron sold his agency in a multi-million-dollar deal to a private equity company. **Now he writes and coaches because he wants to help others live a life they love.**

Notes

Chapter 1:

Avildsen, J. (Director). (1976). *Rocky* [Film]. United Artists.

Dean Bokhari, & Hey, D. B. @DeanBokhari. (2023, February 22). *Action Leads To Motivation (Not The Other Way Around).* Dean Bokhari Website. https://www.deanbokhari.com/acton-leads-motivation/

American Psychological Association. (2018, June). *The Science of Motivation.* American Psychological Association. https://www.apa.org/science/about/psa/2018/06/motivation

Souders, B. (2023, April 24). *Motivation And What Really Drives Human Behavior.* PositivePsychology.com. https://positivepsychology.com/motivation-human-behavior/#emotion

Chapter 2:

Addams, C. (1938). *The Addams Family.* The New Yorker.

Saturday Night Live. (2004, May 1). Episode 18.

Ana The Distracted Gardner. (2020, November 22). Twitter. https://twitter.com/annastayshaa

Kane, B. (1939, May). Detective Comics, Issue #27.

SCL Health. (2019, June). *The Real Health Benefits of Smiling and Laughing.* https://www.sclhealth.org/blog/2019/06/the-real-health-benefits-of-smiling-and-laughing/

Bergland, C. (2012, November 29). *The Neurochemicals Of Happiness*. Psychology Today. https://www.psychologytoday.com/us/blog/the-athletes-way/201211/the-neurochemicals-happiness

Pappas, S., & Harvey, A. (2022, October 6). *Oxytocin: Facts About The Cuddle Hormone*. LiveScience. https://www.livescience.com/42198-what-is-oxytocin.html

Davidson, K. (2023, April 10). *Endorphins: Functions, Levels, And Natural Boosts*. Healthline. https://www.healthline.com/health/endorphins#symptoms

Chapter 3

Lucas, G. (Director). (1977). *Star Wars* [Film]. Twentieth Century Fox.

Addair, G. (n.d.). *The Omega Vector.* https://theomegavector.org/

Pugle, M. (2023, March 25). *How To Retrain Your Thinking And Stop Catastrophizing*. Verywell Health. https://www.verywellhealth.com/managing-anxiety-and-catastrophic-thinking-5192375

Zorbas, A. (2023, May 23). *Personalization: A Common Type Of Negative Thinking*. Therapy Now SF. https://www.therapy-nowsf.com/blog/personalization-a-common-type-of-negative-thinking#:~:text=Personalization%20is%20the%20belief%20that,which%20they%20have%20no%20responsibility

Bernhard, T. (2020, August 20). *It's Time To Stop Taking Things Personally*. Psychology Today. https://www.psychologytoday.com/us/blog/turning-straw-gold/201808/its-time-stop-taking-things-personally

Cuncic, A. (2021, June 25). *Spotlight Effect: Not Everyone Is Looking At You*. Verywell Mind. https://www.verywellmind.com/what-is-the-spotlight-effect-3024470

Spotlight Effect. The Decision Lab. (n.d.). https://thedecisionlab.com/biases/spotlight-effect

Chapter 4

Fleas in a jar experiment, associated with the principles of operant conditioning (attributed to B.F. Skinner).

Chapter 5

Tolle, E. (2006). *A New Earth: Awakening to Your Life's Purpose*. Chivers Press.

Donney, L. (2021, February 26). *Previously On*. *WandaVision*. Season 1, Episode 8, Disney+.

Harvard Health Publishing. (2021, August 14). *Giving Thanks Can Make You Happier*. Harvard Health Publishing. https://www.health. harvard.edu/healthbeat/giving-thanks-can-make-you-happier

UC Davis Health, Public Affairs & Marketing. (2015). *Gratitude Is Good Medicine*. UC Davis Health. https://health.ucdavis.edu/medicalcenter/ features/2015-2016/11/20151125_gratitude.html

Morin, A. (2015, April 3). *7 Scientifically Proven Benefits of Gratitude*. Psychology Today. https://www.psychologytoday.com/us/blog/ what-mentally-strong-people-dont-do/201504/7-scientifical-ly-proven-benefits-gratitude

Ramis, H. (Director) (1993). *Groundhog Day* [Film]. Columbia Pictures.

Chapter 6

Ackerman, C. (2018, March 24). *Learned Helplessness: Seligman's Theory Of Depression*. PositivePsychology.com. https://positivepsychology.com/learned-helplessness-seligman -theory-depression-cure/

Chapter 8

Guest, C. (Director). (2000). *Best In Show* [Film]. Warner Brothers.

Viorst, J., & Cruz, R. (1972). *Alexander And The Terrible, Horrible, No Good, Very Bad Day*. (Reading Rainbow, 14.). Atheneum.

Chapter 9

Shaw, G.B. *Man and Superman*. (1903).

Borgonovi, F. (2008, June 1). *Doing Well By Doing Good. The Relationship Between Formal Volunteering And Self-Reported Health And Happiness.* LSE Research Online. http://eprints.lse.ac.uk/24592/

Chapter 10

Koji, M. (2022, June 9). *The Most Common Workplace Distractions and Tips on How to Tackle Them.* Clockify Blog. https://clockify.me/blog/productivity/workplace-distractions/.

Nauen, R. (2017, July 5). *Over Half Of Employers Lose 1-2 Hours Of Productivity A Day.* CareerBuilder. https://resources.careerbuilder.com/news-research/employers-battle-workforce-distraction

Chapter 11

Stanborough, R. J. (2020, October 2). *Hedonic Treadmill: How Does It Affect Your Happiness?.* Healthline. https://www.healthline.com/health/hedonic-treadmill#types-of-happiness.

Bryne, D. (1985). *Road to Nowhere* [Recorded by Talking Heads].

Brown, E. (Director) (2018). *The Science of Happiness* [Film]. Java Films and Good Giraffe.

Willroth, E., John, O., Biesanz, J., & Mauss, I. (2020, July). *Understanding Short-Term Variability In Life Satisfaction: The Individual Differences In Evaluating Life Satisfaction (IDELS) Model.* Journal Of Personality And Social Psychology. https://www.ncbi.nlm.nih.gov/pmc/articles/PMC7050397/

Power Of Positivity. Facebook. (2022). https://www.facebook.com/powerofpositivity/

Zemeckis, R. (Director) (1994). *Forrest Gump* [Film]. Paramount Pictures.

Chapter 12

Segar, E. C. (1929). *Popeye The Sailor Man.* Thimble Theatre.

Shapiro, D. (2017, March 7). *Negotiating The Nonnegotiable: How To Resolve Your Most Emotionally Charged Conflicts.* Penguin Books.

Eckel, M. D. (2002). *Buddhism: Origins, Beliefs, Practices, Holy Texts, Sacred Places*. Oxford University Press.

McDowell, E. (2022). Instagram @emilyonlife. https://www.instagram.com/emilyonlife/

Gillespie, C. (Director). (2021). *Cruella* [Film]. Walt Disney Studios.

Urminsky, O., & Bartels, D. (2019, December 5). *Chapter 15: Identity, Personal Continuity And Psychological Connectedness Across Time And Over Transformation*. Elgar Online: The Online Content Platform For Edward Elgar Publishing. https://doi.org/10.4337/978178 8117739.00026

Chapter 13

Horton, L. (2019, August 8). *The Neuroscience Behind Our Words*. BRM Institute. https://brm.institute/neuroscience-behind-words/

Richter, M., Eck, J., Straube, T., Miltner, W., & Weiss, T. (2009, October 28). *Do Words Hurt? Brain Activation During the Processing of Pain-Related Words*. ScienceDirect. https://www.sciencedirect.com/science/article/abs/pii/S0304395909004564

Lynch, B. (Director). (2015). *Minons* [Film]. Universal Studios.

Lodge, J., Harte, D. K., & Tripp, G. (1998, March). *Children's Self-Talk Under Conditions of Mild Anxiety*. Journal of Anxiety Disorders. https://pubmed.ncbi.nlm.nih.gov/9560177/

Newberg, A. B., & Waldman, M. R. (2013). *Words Can Change Your Brain: 12 Conversation Strategies to Build Trust, Resolve Conflict, and Increase Intimacy*. Plume.

Kid, C. (2019, September 28). *100+ Funny Self-Deprecating Quotes and Caption Ideas*. TurboFuture. https://turbofuture.com/internet/Funny-Self-Deprecating-Caption-Ideas.

Chapter 14

ABC. (1987, September 28). *Full House*. Episode 1.

Tabitha. (2022). Facebook Page *The Real Healing*. https://www.facebook.com/therealhealing

Brenner, A. (2020, January 29). *7 Strategies to Put the Past Behind You.* Psychology Today. Sussex Publishers. https://www.psychologytoday. com/us/blog/in-flux/202001/7-strategies-put-the-past-behind-you

Chapter 15

Rolling Stones. (1969, July 4). *You Can't Always Get What You Want.* Jagger, M. and Richards, K. (Writers). Miller, J. (Producer).

Carrey, J. (2014, May 30). *Commencement Address.* Maharishi International University of Management.

Santayana, G. (1910). *Three Philosophical Poets.* Harvard University.

Graham, B. (2000). *The Holy Spirit: Activating God's Power In Your Life.* Thomas Nelson.

NBC. (2005, March 24). *The Office.* Episode 1.

Chapter 16

Liman. D. (Director). (2014). *Edge of Tomorrow* [Film]. Warner Bros.

Carroll, L. (1893). *Alice's Adventures in Wonderland.* T. Y. Crowell & Co.

Wiest, B. (2016). *101 Essays That Will Change the Way You Think.* Thought Catalog Books.

Chapter 17

Cutfort, D. and Lipsitz, J. (2022, March 18). *Is It Cake?* Episode 1, Netflix.

Ivan, K. (1814). *The Inquisitive Man.* J. Wrigley

100 Things You Can Do to Save the Planet. Sierra Club. (n.d.). https:// www.sierraclub.org/toiyabe/100-things-you-can-do-save-planet

Pimentel, D., & Pimentel, M. (2003, September). *Sustainability of Meat-Based and Plant-Based Diets and the Environment.* The American Journal Of Clinical Nutrition. https://academic.oup.com/ ajcn/article/78/3/660S/4690010

Conzachi, K. (2022, March 16). *It May Be Uncomfortable, But We Need To Talk About It: The Animal Agriculture Industry and Zero Waste*. University of Colorado Boulder. https://www.colorado.edu/ecenter/2022/03/15/it-may-be-uncomfortable-we-need-talk-about-it-animal-agriculture-industry-and-zero-waste

Metz, C. (2023, May 1). *What Exactly Are The Dangers Posed by A.I.?* The New York Times. https://www.nytimes.com/2023/05/01/technology/ai-problems-danger-chatgpt.html

www.ingramcontent.com/pod-product-compliance
Lightning Source LLC
Chambersburg PA
CBHW062105080426
42734CB00012B/2754